The Art of Change

Faith, Vision, *and* Prophetic Planning

John Reid
and Maureen Gallagher
From The Reid Group

Liguori
LIGUORI, MISSOURI

Imprimi Potest:
Thomas D. Picton, C.Ss.R.
Provincial, Denver Province
The Redemptorists

Published by Liguori Publications
Liguori, Missouri
To order, call 800-325-9521
www.liguori.org

Library of Congress Cataloging-in-Publication Data

Reid, J. M. (John M.), 1948-
    The art of change : faith, vision, and prophetic planning / John Reid and Maureen Gallagher. — 1st ed.
        p. cm.
    ISBN 978-0-7648-1867-7
    1. Change—Religious aspects—Christianity. 2. Planning. 3. Leadership—Religious aspects—Christianity. I. Gallagher, Maureen, 1938- II. Title.
    BV4509.5.R446 2009
    254—dc22

2009029653

Additional copyright acknowledgments are in the Acknowledgments section, page 116.

Liguori Publications, a nonprofit corporation, is an apostolate of the Redemptorists. To learn more about the Redemptorists, visit Redemptorists.com.

Printed in the United States of America
13 12 11 10 09   5 4 3 2 1
First edition

JOHN REID has worked with the Archdiocese of Seattle for 18 years where he had responsibilities for formation, training, and placement for lay and ordained ministers and was also Coordinator of Transition Services. John has given talks and workshops nationally on leadership, collaboration, and transition. Besides working in diocesan planning and ministries, his consulting services include work within healthcare, higher education, and government.

MAUREEN GALLAGHER has more than 25 years experience in leadership, planning, facilitation, and organizational development. She has worked for the Diocese of Madison and the Archdiocese of Milwaukee in the areas of planning, parish, school, and educational leadership. She has consulted with communities of women religious, taught, and been an administrator at the university level. She has created educational and planning materials for faith-based and non-profit organizations.

THE REID GROUP has developed a wide range of programs and workshops to help leaders and organizations transform challenges into opportunities to create a better world. They provide comprehensive services to build teams and community (www.thereidgroup.biz). John and Maureen are partners with The Reid Group.

To J. Gordon Myers
for his inspiration, leadership,
and for being a great colleague
in helping leaders and groups
plan for their futures.

Contents

CHAPTER 8

Creating a Culture of Prophetic Planning
and Effective Action ■ 89

CHAPTER 9

Pulling It All Together—A Spiritual Journey ■ 101

Resources ■ 113

Acknowledgments ■ 116

Introduction

EVERY ORGANIZATION has a past and a present. While this may be self-evident, it is also true that every existing organization is not guaranteed to continue indefinitely. The future must be prepared for, worked for, and created by leaders and others committed to the organization. The future is rooted in the past and built upon the present. Even when organizations have served their original purpose and may no longer need to exist, a plan needs to be developed. Such a plan will honor the past and determine how the values of the past and present can be respected and appreciated in the future.

The Art of Change: Faith, Vision, and Prophetic Planning is written to assist leaders and their colleagues to be creative, effective, and bold in envisioning their organization's future and to be practical, successful, and results-oriented in bringing the vision to life in positive and constructive ways. Planning is a journey. It is a spiritual journey, a hope-filled one, a social one, an intellectual one, and one that often results in physical changes to organizations.

We at The Reid Group have had the privilege of helping many organizations plan their futures over the past twelve years. In his book *The Fifth Discipline,* Peter Senge says that another word for planning is learning. As we work with various groups, we become part of their learning communities, adjusting, adapting, creating, and walking with them on their planning journey. This book is the result of The Reid Group team's cumulative experience of over a hundred years of leading groups in designing their futures. We are sharing what we have learned by working with archbishops, bishops, priests, deacons, religious and lay leaders as staff in the Archdiocese of Seattle, the Archdiocese of Milwaukee, and in many other dioceses, religious communities, nonprofit organizations, and other settings. We hope that you will join us on the planning journey and share your insights with us and each other on our blog: www.TheReidGroup.biz.

As planning consultants, we continue our planning journey with many faith-based, nonprofit, and for-profit organizations. We believe that planning processes are special times of learning, creativity, and new life for organizations. Organizational planning helps establish a preferred or favored direction for an organization in the face of many possibilities.

The proper end of a planning process is the state where clarity exists around answers to some key questions: What are we about? Where are we heading? Why are we doing what we are doing? How will we achieve our goals? Who will be involved? When will all the work take place? Who is responsible for what actions?

A successful planning process is designed to help an organization clarify where it is going as it moves forward into the future. The process helps organizations identify their focus and priorities for the next few years. An effective planning process will build on the strengths of the present and will also provide opportunities for participation by many individuals and groups.

For Whom Is This Book Written?

This book is written for leaders of change. It is written for both individuals and organizations. The planning principles and processes described in *The Art of Change: Faith, Vision, and Prophetic Planning* can easily be used by any profit, nonprofit, government, or faith-based organization interested in successful planning. Many of the examples and suggested enriching experiences are based on a broad range of Judeo-Christian beliefs, Scriptures, symbols, and rituals that have been experienced in various dioceses, parishes, schools and colleges, health care organizations, communities of vowed religious, other faith-based organizations, and nonprofits.

Fundamental to the Prophetic Planning processes found in this book is the virtue of hope. The goal of hope is not survival, but a flourishing organization. Hope says change can provide fertile ground for new life. Hope is rooted in the life-death-resurrection mystery of Christ and is found in the fullness of life. Hope, as embedded in the planning process, creates what can hardly be imagined in the present.

The renowned German theologian, Jürgen Moltmann, reminds us that hope and planning are interconnected. It is impossible to successfully have one without the other. "Unless hope has been roused and is alive, there can be no stimulation for planning. Without specific goals towards which hope is directed...there can be no realistic hope." This book is about creating from challenges, change, and loss a hope-filled future where life can be fully experienced.

There are nine chapters in this book, plus a list of resources for Prophetic Planners. All the chapters focus on different parts of the Prophetic Planning journey.

CHAPTER ONE

"A Case for Prophetic Planning" describes the framework for Prophetic Planning and its four foundational pillars. It points to a journey that needs participation from those who will be impacted by the results of the plan. It highlights the need for crafting clear statements of mission, values, vision, goals, and objectives. The chapter addresses the need to deal with the real issues the organization is facing, as well as ongoing monitoring and evaluation of the plan.

CHAPTER TWO

"Change and Transformation" presents a model for dealing with change, especially noting the main part of the journey is through the wilderness zone. In between endings and new beginnings, one must cross through the "wilderness zone" of uncertainty, chaos, fear, and anxiety. Much as the Israelites had to spend forty years in the desert, or Jesus forty days in wilderness, so too planners need to be aware that there is no straight and easy road to new beginnings. However, we have learned how to live in and move across the wilderness from those who have gone before us, from good social science research, and from how we celebrate our faith and values through ritual and storytelling.

CHAPTER THREE

"Conflict Management and Resistance to Change" deals with the reality that when you are on a planning journey building the future, it is impossible to avoid all conflict and resistance to change. Conflict is part of daily life. If everyone thought alike all the time, life would be boring and creativity would be at a standstill. Differences are not the issue. How we deal with them is what is significant. Being a successful conflict manager means being a good communicator and being able to mediate differences. It includes knowing how to deal with anger, hostility, and pain. Good facilitators of conflict are respectful of differences, do not take sides, and can de-escalate emotional situations with well-honed listening skills and the ability to help people use a variety of problem-solving strategies.

CHAPTER FOUR

"The Role of Faith and Values in the Prophetic Planning Process" helps people reflect upon planning with the eyes of faith on the journey. It calls for an understanding of the current reality, building on the common good, and discovering what prophets and planners have in common. This chapter gives examples of values found in health care, Catholic schools, parishes, and nonprofit organizations.

CHAPTER FIVE

"Envisioning the Future" focuses on looking at the role vision plays in the overall planning journey and suggests three visioning processes. Two draw primarily on the imagination and guide people to imagine what the next five years will look like if all the hopes and dreams of the group are realized. The third, scenario planning, is more analytical and approaches the visioning exercise using data and a lot of "What ifs." These three visioning processes have been used successfully with groups around the country.

CHAPTER SIX

"Dealing with Grief and Loss" are part of planning journeys. The signs of grieving such as numbness and panic, nostalgia and protests, discouragement and disorientation, are described along with ways to help groups move forward, especially by assisting them to realize all the things that are not changing. Processes are discussed which help people move through the wilderness journey from endings to new beginnings.

CHAPTER SEVEN

"Conversation—the Foundation of Prophetic Planning" points to three different ways to journey with *The Art of Change.* One, using the "Eight Steps Process," is successful for large organizations with satellites such as dioceses with parishes and nonprofits with branch offices. It involves using conversation and dialogue throughout the process. The second model is a "Retreat Model," which calls leaders (sixty to eighty of them or more) together to provide a positive and collective energy with new ideas and wisdom for the plan. It uses surveys throughout the process (hard copy and Internet links) to get input from all constituencies such as parishioners, parents of Catholic school children, and so forth. This model is ideal for parish, school, or nonprofit planning that does not involve multiple entities. The third process is the "Appreciative Scenario" process. It combines elements of appreciative inquiry with scenario building and has been used successfully with faith-based nonprofits and communities of vowed religious.

CHAPTER EIGHT

"Creating a Culture of Prophetic Planning and Effective Action" reflects upon culture—the need for a culture of planning as well as the need to understand culture and diversity to do Prophetic Planning. Explorations of concepts such as co-cultures are explored and applied to both individuals and organizations.

CHAPTER NINE

"Pulling It All Together—A Spiritual Journey" leads people to reflect on the Prophetic Planning journey. Learnings are explored in five areas: Openness to Mystery; Prophetic Planning as a Continual Process; Stresses Along the Way; Connecting Along the Way; and Seeing, Naming, and Acting, which are at the heart of successful planning. The journey is often one of loss and grief as well as joy and hope.

RESOURCES

This section provides a bibliography of helpful planning resources, many of which are referred to in this book, as well as multi-media resources for use with groups in the planning processes suggested.

CHAPTER **1**

A Case for Prophetic Planning

To be both prophetic and public, a countersign to much of the culture, but also a light and leaven for all of it, is the delicate balance to which we are called.

JOSEPH CARDINAL BERNARDIN,
THE LATE CARDINAL ARCHBISHOP OF CHICAGO

A WISE PERSON ONCE NOTED: "To fail to plan is to plan to fail." To be able to say this genuinely, the wisdom figure first must have experienced the positive benefits of a successful planning process in his or her life. Certainly, no one wants to fail. Yet, many leaders seem reluctant to embrace the art and science of planning as a key strategy for success in their work life and beyond.

The biblical passage reminds us that "Where there is no prophecy, the people cast off restraint..."(Proverbs 29:18). Vision and imagination are at the heart of planning. The possibilities are practically endless when planning groups are brought together in a spirit of openness, realism, curiosity, and creativity. Just a few of the benefits found in saying "yes" to being proactive about the future include the following:

- You have the opportunity to think together with colleagues about creative and practical ways of helping your parish, school, diocese, or nonprofit company move beyond the status quo of the present into the future.

■ You can finally focus the energy of a critical mass of leaders in your organization on the pressing issues that drain way too much energy—whether these be issues of mission and vision, financing, staffing, facilities, or internal and external relationships. Now is the time to address these critical issues and respond to them.

■ You will be energized. As the old saying goes, "The more you are involved in the process, the more you will be committed to the outcome." As the commitment level to a new future increases, so does the energy to "make it happen."

■ You and your colleagues will be empowered to think and act together with "one voice" rather than responding with many individual voices, and so you will make a bigger impact, have more influence, and garner more ownership.

Given these and other benefits from participating in creative and effective planning processes, why is it that leaders at times seem to have limited or no commitment to organization-wide planning initiatives? Several valid reasons come to mind:

■ Poor experience with planning efforts in the past; significant resources were devoted to planning processes with limited results; "the new plan wound up on the shelf."

■ Planning for some indicates a lack of confidence in the leaders; some say that it is the leaders' task to chart the future, not the whole organization's task.

■ Planning processes can at times seem to last forever and not lead to specific and practical outcomes. In other words, there is too much focus on planning and not nearly enough positive action toward implementation.

■ Planning is just not much fun for some; it can be tedious and even full of conflict.

For a high commitment to quality, productive, and meaningful planning, these factors must be addressed. Planning, if done well, can transform churches, schools, congregations of religious, health care institutions, adult learning centers, and all organizations into renewed vibrant entities. This does not mean that there will not be change and loss in the process. Some things may need to die for rebirth to happen. A significant belief underlying *The Art of Change* is that effective planning can transform organizations, communities, and beyond into the wider world. For a positive "culture of planning" to take root in organizations, the issues stated above must honestly and directly be recognized and attended to.

Not Just Any Old Planning

In order to examine some of the reasons people resist planning, well thought-out planning processes which lead to desired results need to be initiated. No one joins an organization or accepts a leadership position to focus all his or her energy on planning. Leaders want to act effectively in order to make a positive difference in their department, parish, school, organization, and community. In this context, planning is appropriately seen as a way to achieve desired or hoped for results—some clearly identified and constructive actions that will chart the future.

In order to achieve the preferred results, certain things need to be in place. There are six key elements for successful planning:

1. Encourage participation by many different people with varying experiences and perspectives on the organization. The more people contribute their own ideas and best thinking—their "handprints and footprints" throughout the planning process—the more the organization will enhance learning, and the more people will become strongly invested in the process.

2. Craft clear statements of mission, values, vision, goals, objectives, and action steps. Talk is cheap, if it is not followed up with action. Statements of mission, values, and the rest can only have the

intended impact if they are rooted in the reality of the organization. These declarations need to inspire people to say something like, "Yes, this is who we are," or "Yes, we can become more like this as we move with confidence into the future."

3. Address important issues facing the organization, for example, staffing, funding, facilities, and relationships. Every organization has issues. These need to be named and addressed. What is the reality the diocese, parish, or nonprofit is facing? How does this affect the future vitality of the people in the group and the organization as a whole? The key here is not just to see or name the critical issues, but to develop a game plan for addressing the issues in ways that strengthen the organization and all those committed to its mission and values.

4. Creatively promote the plan as a living document. Plans are road maps to the future and provide tremendous opportunities to educate the "shareholders" of an organization about the newly articulated mission, values, vision, and goals. Whether they are parishioners, parents, students, health care patients, or anyone who uses the services of the organization, they will welcome an opportunity to see what the organization believes about itself and what it hopes to accomplish.

5. Focus on the transition from a planning process to an action-oriented implementation process. Some of the cynicism often associated with planning comes from plans that are bound in attractive covers but which stay in drawers and never see action. The movement toward implementation with timelines and named responsibilities is as important as the planning process. A truncated plan is no plan at all.

6. Regularly evaluate and update the plan and its implementation. Initially the evaluations are appropriately done at three or six-month intervals. Once the plan is established, annual assessments and updates are integral to thriving implementation. The most successful implementation processes are those where the action steps of the plan are incorporated into performance evaluations.

This includes both board performance, if the actions call for board involvement, or staff/volunteer performance assessments.

When all six of these elements are implemented, the investment of work, time, and money required to plan well create the foundation for a significant and abundant dividend of thinking together, quality planning, and constructive action.

Why Prophetic Planning?

Even when the elements outlined above are in place, the question still remains as to exactly what kind of planning process will be implemented. Prophetic Planning does not promote timid, status quo or risk-free planning. Rather, it embraces an exciting and creative approach. This approach invites organizational leaders, and indeed everyone who participates in the planning process, to be bold and proactive in creating a new and vital future for the organization they care so much about. Father George Wilson, SJ, in his short pamphlet "On Being a Prophet," says that "a prophet sees what's happening in what's happening." Father Wilson goes on to say : "Hearing prophets has to do with being hospitable. That's not easy. Hospitality doesn't mean simply playing the role of a host. It involves a radical openness to all the ways the divine chooses to come and to speak to us…including prophets who may not look or act in ways that are inviting. That kind of openness isn't easy. It is painful and involves forms of death. God comes to us in forms we don't expect."

Thus, for planners to be prophetic in a deep sense of the word, they must not only see what is happening around them, they must also possess a radical openness—to God's actions and to the voices, perspectives, questions, and insights of everyone involved in the planning process, "including prophets who may not look or act in ways that are inviting."

There are four essential elements to Prophetic Planning:

1. Planning for the future is based on knowledge and appreciation for the story of the organization that has evolved from the past.

2. The realities of faith, conversion, and healing are central to quality planning and effective organizational development.

3. While appreciating what has been, this approach to planning invites leaders to be bold and ask questions like, "What would we do if we were ten times bolder?" and "What would we do if we REALLY considered ourselves a FOR PROPHET organization?"

4. Prophetic Planning seeks to discern the movement of the Spirit and the will of God for an organization at this moment in time.

The Past

The past in any organization MATTERS a great deal. While organizations can't move into the future when living in the past, it is also true that they will experience many obstacles to future opportunities if they try to ignore or discount the importance of the past. As someone wisely stated, "The past is always good for two things—to recall good memories and to learn from." Organizations that remember and celebrate their past with pride and that honor their traditions and rituals learn much from their history and are empowered to build on a strong foundation as they work together to create a bright new future.

One organization involved in a planning process wondered if its existence in the United States might have accomplished its mission and if it should go out of existence and give its assets to a third world country where the organization was needed and was just beginning to thrive. The thinking was that its mission might never be vibrant in the United States given the cultural transformation since its founding, but there was a sense of honor and pride that the organization might thrive on another continent with the cherished assets present here. This is prophetic thinking!

Three parishes that were going to share a pastor decided, through prayer, discussion among the councils, and many parish meetings, to ask the bishop for permission to merge. In the process, they realized each of their churches was too small to effectively use for Sunday Eucharist of the newly-formed community. A farmer came forward and suggested: "What if I donated land, and we built a new church and parish complex?" In the process of acknowledging a great deal of loss—buildings built through the sacrifice of grandparents and great grandparents—and through celebrating the stories of the past, the parishes took a prophetic stance. With the encouragement of the bishop, they built a new complex that not only served the Catholic community, but also was available for other community groups.

Faith, Conversion, and Healing

All organizations have particular beliefs, including convictions that flow from personal and collective faith as well as from shared values and vision. At risk organizations ignore what they share in common with others or fail to capitalize on the faith and values that are shared. Similarly, the status quo can only last so long. Therefore, insightful planners regularly look to tried and true ways of growing and changing.

Conversion is the faith word for change. Transformation is the change word that well describes what occurs in any values-based organization. In either case, conversion and change represent an opportunity to move forward with positive energy and dynamism from the current reality or status quo of today to a bright new future tomorrow.

Just as each person needs healing at times, so healing needs to occur consistently within organizations and within the life shared by leaders and followers alike. Important questions to consider in this area include:

■ Who is hurting in our group or in our larger organization?

■ Whose voice is not at the table when key decisions are made?

■ Who is not being empowered right here and right now?

■ What can we do individually and collectively to facilitate inner and outer healing and help folks let go of baggage from the past so they can contribute so much more to the future?

In one planning effort, the group could not move forward because of some unresolved past issues. It was not until the "elephant" in the room was named that the group had the power to send the elephant away and get on with preparing for the future. When the elephant started to appear in the room again, it could be named and "sent out to pasture" again. Naming the unresolved issues and beginning to deal with them liberated the group to be productive. Seeing, naming, and acting regarding "elephants" is part of Prophetic Planning. It is a way to experience conversion and healing.

Being Bold

Planning times are not times to be bashful or timid. Rather, they are exciting times when boldness and a prophetic spirit are required. Two questions that elicit boldness are:

1. What would we do if we were ten times bolder? If we…would we…? What if…?
2. What would we look like in the future if we REALLY considered ourselves a "for-prophet" organization and lived deeply the *prophetic* reality?

One nonprofit planning group was struggling with competition from other professional groups who were having success with cooperative efforts. The question arose about joining the collaborative work. The fear of loss of identity became an initial obstacle to aligning in partnership with other groups. Gradually, through some "What if…?" prophetic thinking, the possibility of joining and maintaining identity began to be explored with amazing results.

In another planning effort related to the need to move from three schools to one using two buildings, "What if…?" prophetic thinking led to being able to use all three buildings—two for elementary education and one for community education. Without the "What if…?" thinking, the experience of how to use resources beyond elementary education would never have produced the community education model.

God's Will

Discerning the movement of the Spirit or God's will is both very important and very hard to measure. Yet, in faith, in prayer, and in communal conversations, striving to discern the Spirit's presence is one of the benchmarks of quality planning. One way to measure or evaluate how well an organization is listening for the movement of the Spirit is to consider the fruits of their actions. Jesus says so powerfully in John's Gospel, "I came that they might have life, and have it abundantly" (John 10:10). Therefore, one way to measure how well an organization is doing in this area is to look for the signs and realities that point to new life. The more life that is being seen, named, and acted upon, the more God's will is being lived out. New life might also be embedded in some death moments. Faith helps planners discover God's presence in all of reality.

The planning efforts of one congregation of religious women whose membership totaled fewer than one hundred sisters and whose average age was in the mid seventies was surprisingly prophetic. Through prayer, discernment, dialogue, and the creation of different scenarios, the sisters were led to consider tearing down buildings to which they were very attached. The venerable structures had great memories. However, they were not meeting the sisters' needs as they got older, and the buildings were consuming exorbitant amounts of energy and thus financial resources. By tearing down the old residences, the sisters were able to build a beautiful, brand new structure that truly met their needs. The new building could be easily converted into public housing for the elderly in the future. When they started the process, they never dreamed that would be the outcome. Prophetic Planning is full of surprises!

Prophetic Planning honors the past, cherishes all the sacrifices that went into making the organization what it has become, recognizes change in terms of faith and the need for conversion and healing, seeks boldness in imagining a future where the mission, values, vision, and goals of the organization can flourish, and strives to discern the presence of God in the planning process.

For Reflection and Discussion

1. What new or renewed insights did you get from reading this chapter?
2. How can Prophetic Planning be a useful process for your organization?
3. Why is it important to honor the past in planning?
4. How do you see "conversion" related to planning?
5. What do you see as the strengths and challenges embedded in Prophetic Planning?

CHAPTER

Change and Transformation

All change results from a change in meaning....Change occurs only when we let go of our certainty, our current views, and develop a new understanding of what's going on.
MARGARET WHEATLEY

PROPHETIC PLANNING helps groups grow stronger during times of change. It strengthens organizations to journey together with strength and courage. It gets to the "heart of the matter." It empowers organizations to use their resources wisely, avoid duplication, and create a new synergy, transforming challenges into opportunities to build a better world.

Change is an inevitable part of life. Learning to manage change on a personal, interpersonal, and organizational level can lead to meaningful transitions. Understanding the overall process of change can prevent individuals and organizations from getting lost in the process or from giving up when some resistance is experienced. Knowing the various factors that affect change and transitions, and understanding the implications of change in personal lives, in relationships, and in structures, builds capacity to manage and lead change. Learning how to connect people in the change process brings meaning and purpose to the transition. It helps people grow stronger in the change process.

11

Life is about changing. We experience personal change often. Sometimes we embrace it. A promotion, a surprise visit, the birth of a child are occasions to celebrate. Sometimes change is imposed from the outside—a job is eliminated or terminated; illness imposes limitations on our activities; the death of a loved one radically changes our lives. Natural disasters can destroy our homes. Seasonal changes may bring about mood swings. New information or technology may bring about drastic changes in how we approach a project. Sometimes we seek to avoid change at all costs.

To choose to change is inherent to leading meaningful lives. We decide where to go to college, what our major will be, what kind of a job we will seek, who we will marry, where we will live, etc. In general, about ten percent of the population welcomes change; another ten percent refuses to change. The remaining eighty percent will fluctuate at any given moment between resisting and embracing change. At times people see change as advantageous and beneficial. They feel it is an opportunity to grow or gain prosperity. At other times they are fearful and anxious about change. They dread it and steer clear of it as much as possible. They live by the maxim, "If it is not broken, don't fix it!"

Change happens on both the personal and interpersonal level. Relationships can be fractured, only to be resolved and become stronger than they were initially. They can also be irreparably broken and need to be ended with as much respect and dignity as possible. As people mature, they often gain knowledge related to managing change. Experience allows people to understand the impact of change and to recognize and avoid some of the stumbling blocks in transitions. Mentors, coaches, mediators, and counselors help individuals and groups transform challenges into positive opportunities. Inherent in transitions are the experiences of loss and grief. All this is part of the transformation process. It is part of the life-death-resurrection mystery that many share as baptized Christians.

Not only does change happen on the personal and interpersonal levels, it happens on the organizational level. Since 1990, forty-five percent of companies in the United States have reduced their work force. Corporations have merged at a fast rate during the last two decades, changing their identities and their mission. The change is sometimes one of growth or one of diminishment, or a little of both. Growth in the development of communication technology has eliminated the need in some instances for cabling and wire connections as society moves toward becoming "wireless." There may be less need for linemen and more need for wireless technicians as the technology world grows. The "super highway" of communicating with the world, a dream in the early 1980s, has become a reality. This has caused the elimination of some jobs and the creation of new ones. The way change is managed in organizations will influence the results, either positively or negatively. Well-managed change leads to stronger organizations.

Many of the mainline Christian denominations have been experiencing change in their membership. Active members are decreasing. Some younger members are questioning the value of "belonging" or of "organized religion" in the twenty-first century. The Catholic Church is a large organization that has been going through change for the last two thousand years. Currently in much of the Western world, the Church is experiencing three important change factors: demographic changes in membership, the availability of priests to serve the communities, and cultural phenomena which question its relevance and viability. These factors have not only affected the institution itself, but also corporations within it such as schools, universities, congregations of men and women religious, and health care organizations.

In government and the nonprofit world, change is also apparent, especially in the allocation of resources. Small fire and police departments are merging to serve larger areas. Public utilities are centralizing to be more financially viable. Organizations such as the American Heart Association have moved to a national structure to avoid duplication and to consolidate resources. Partnerships or collaboratives are becoming more common between similar service-oriented nonprofits. Working together increases sustainability and has a greater impact.

Endings, New Beginnings, the Wilderness Zone

ENDINGS	WILDERNESS ZONE	NEW BEGINNINGS

Change is about endings and new beginnings. Endings point to loss—often the loss of something of great value to a person, to a relationship, or to an organization. Perhaps a job is gone, a relationship is jeopardized, a building is not used, a comfort zone is not available. Possibly there is a loss of confidence, health, marketable skills, and potential earning power. At the other end of the spectrum are the new beginnings such as fresh relationships, greater opportunities, successful negotiations, new technology, all of which open the door to unimagined prospects and possibilities.

In between the two ends of the spectrum there is the "wilderness." Moses and the Israelites spent forty years in the wilderness. They searched for food, water, comforts of home. It was a very difficult time for them. They were called to trust and hope that God was leading them to a better place, which turned out to be the Promised Land. Jesus spent forty days in the desert after his baptism in the Jordan, preparing for his public ministry and resisting temptations along the way.

No one wants to spend much time in the wilderness. It is a place of uncertainty, fear, anxiety. It is a time of disruption. All the things one counts on are up for grabs. The wilderness zone is the "in between time." It is when people journey from the known into the unknown, from certainty into the messiness of uncertainty. It is a mysterious period, a puzzlement, a time to question what will be. Planning is the process of helping individuals and organizations cross the desert or find the way out of the wilderness. Working productively in the wilderness zone provides opportunities for individuals and organizations to grow stronger and to have a renewed understanding of who they are and who they are called to be.

The Catholic Church as an organization is experiencing change, which affects a great many parishioners. Due to changing demographics, the diminishing number of priests, and limited financial resources, many dioceses have entered into a comprehensive parish planning process. Many parishioners identify the Church with a building. In some cases, it is a structure that their great grandparents helped build by making tremendous personal sacrifices. The faith of the people is often intertwined on some level with the church structure. They may even be attached to the family pew—where they always sit! The traditions and memories of the parish can be a great building block for the future, or they can become an obstacle. Managing change well can lead to stronger more committed parishioners. Having a well thought-out process and involving them in the process is the key to success.

In order to help people and organizations through the wilderness, opportunities should be provided to enable them to interact with others, to ask questions, to take a part in creating the change. All of this will lessen their resistance. This is most effective when they are invited to converse with the community and come to new understandings. It is a process. No one leader, no matter how charismatic, can lead change alone. No one person has all the wisdom to help a community grow stronger in the midst of change. What is needed is an engaging process, which can encourage an exchange of attitudes, beliefs, skills, capabilities, perceptions, and new visions. Such processes will lead to a new level of commitment. Change in parish or other cherished structures often touches upon the core beliefs of people and gives them an opportunity to examine what is at the heart of the matter, what is truly important and life-giving.

Frequently, people who are able to cope with change in their family life and in their professions draw the line when it comes to faith. Faith is a bedrock. It is a stable force in people's lives. When all else changes, faith is suppose to remain the same and be a constant. In reality, faith is the constant; it is life-giving; it promises hope; it sustains people in the wilderness. However, for this to happen, faith needs to be somewhat disengaged from a particular building or a particular community. Although we can acknowledge that specific churches and communities fostered an individual's and a family's faith and may continue to do so, for growth to occur, faith needs to be seen as more expansive than a particular building or group of people.

Faith also grows and changes. It never remains stagnant. Changes in church structures often are invitations to grow in faith—to discover the heart of the matter. What is changing? What is staying the same?

In all change, the core values of the organization are often what are not changing. In congregations of religious men and women who are undergoing drastic migration in membership, and consequently in the kinds of ministry possibilities available, the core values are often what are not changing. Age factors and numbers of members may diminish the work of the community, but the faith, core identity, and values of the community often remain a constant.

Prophetic Planning involves developing practices and tools which will serve the community for many years. Given the opportunities for involvement in evaluating the current quality of ministries and in suggesting changes for the future, people will gain confidence and be empowered to deal with losses, as well as to create exciting futures. The involvement of the people affected by change in the process ensures high quality results and ownership, which pave the way to success. The following diagram illustrates an effective way to manage the transition process and move toward personal, relational, and organizational transformation.

Transition Process

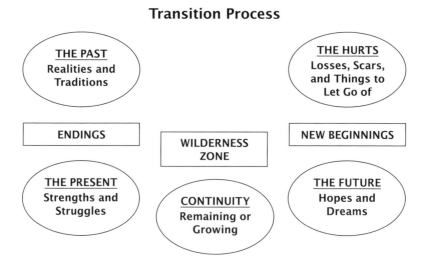

The Past—Realities and Traditions

Planning, whether focused on the work of nonprofits, governments, faith-based organizations, or churches, always begins with the current realities. Max DePree, a successful CEO of a Fortune 500 company, defines the role of the leader in the change process as one who does four things. The first is that the leader defines reality; the last is that the leader says "thank you." In between, the leader is a servant and a debtor. Seeing oneself as a servant, as facilitating transitions, is an energizing image. Being indebted to relationships or the organization with which one is working and serving liberates one from feeling the total responsibility of "solving all the planning issues" raised in the process; it provides the sustained vigor to stay aligned with the transition process, even when it becomes very difficult.

Reality is always changing. Often there is a shift in demographics, or in the new perceived needs of the community or organization, or in diminishing resources, aging membership, and so forth. These can bring anxiety, questioning, and concerns. Something always triggers the awareness of the need to plan for change. This is not always negative. Sometimes it is an innovative product or service that needs a marketing plan, which starts a major planning process. The development of a plan and strategy can be very rewarding, because it may open new doors and stir the imagination to dream in a way that could never have been predicted.

Both remembering and celebrating the past are important building blocks for the future. Storytelling and gathering symbols or artifacts associated with the past are often helpful ways to connect with what has gone before and to realize the profound gift the past has been. Beginning with questions such as "When in the past were we at our best? What are the gifts upon which we can build? What will carry us forward from the past into the future?" are all ways to link past and present experience in a way that helps people articulate expectations for the future. The storytelling and sharing of symbols often bring both tears and gales of laughter. The process itself has healing attributes.

The articulation and sharing of traditions is important in any kind of organizational "coming together." Mergers, whether you are talking about consolidating parishes, provinces of a religious community, volunteer fire departments, or regional areas of Boy Scouts or Girl Scouts, provide multiple opportunities to communicate particular traditions. In so doing, barriers are broken down and the new organization has additional ways to bond and celebrate its new existence. Many traditions can continue even when buildings are sold, fire stations closed, communities of religious amalgamated, or scouting troops brought together. The great traditions of the organizations can continue to nurture communities despite the disruption of time and place.

The Present—Strengths and Struggles

Looking at the present, knowing that it is not sustainable, can be disturbing. Until individuals and organizations are willing to embrace the difficulty of uncertainties, they will not be able to effectively deal with change. It is hard to give up certainties, particular ways of doing things, or meaningful activities.

Facing change, however, forces us to listen well, stand in the shoes of another, think with others, and design the future together. The future is based on the strengths of each organization, each parish, each health care institution, each school, and so forth, when engaging in significant conversations. It involves rich dialogue about what the strengths of each are and what the challenges and struggles are. Planning is about more than just problem solving; it is about building relationships, partnerships, creating new possibilities, discovering gifts, planting seeds—designing a new tapestry which will serve tomorrow well.

Inviting people into conversation to share what is important to them, hearing all voices, and valuing differences are effective ways to begin dealing with the change process. It takes faith, courage, and patience to have purposeful conversations. Powerful questions need to be asked. We need to talk about what we really care about. Dialoguing is a natural way of thinking together. It means we must slow down and reflect. As Christ challenged Martha to relax and not be concerned about the "nitty gritty," so we must confront ourselves to be focused about the really important things in life. The small stuff will always be there and have the power to drain our energy and cloud our vision for what really brings us new life. Christ believed Martha could appreciate the bigger picture of trying to build the reign of God. Christ is challenging us to be bold and focus on what is really important.

In the nonprofit world where religious imagery and faith may not be appropriate frameworks, the same process of meaningful conversation and dialogue can be situated in good social science research. This points to the skills involved in respectful dialogue, owning feelings, avoiding "blaming language," discerning the values that need to be preserved, and articulating hopes, dreams, and cherished outcomes. Appropriate stories from the heroes and heroines of history and/or literature can be effective tools to help groups see the bigger picture and to understand how others have coped with change, transition, loss and new life. In the nonprofit world, the underlying value for planning and changes is the common good.

The Hurts—Losses, Scars, and Letting Go of Things

In dealing with change, nothing is more powerful than helping communities discover what is really significant to them. The consequence of this is threefold. First, the shared meaning around loss helps bond those who will become a new community. Second, when loss occurs, a larger group than the one most deeply affected will be available for support and understanding. Third, the loss may be understood in a new, more life-giving way through meaningful conversations.

Loss occurs when great people will no longer be available to serve a particular group. It may start with people speaking about a venerable person: a pastor, scout leader, executive director, or leader in any organization. Gradually people will start conversing about missing certain artifacts, the stained glass windows, the statues, the scout room the troop painted, the old novitiate or motherhouse, the bell tower, and so on.

The closing of one small church brought great consternation because there was a large round window in the back which had an eye portrayed in an artistic fashion. From the time they were small, children were told that the eye was the "eye of God," and that God was watching over all the people who came to church. The reinforcement of the stained glass window being the eye of God was so strong that people mourned the loss of the window as if they were losing their relationship with God. Through conversation with the community, more people began to realize the great significance of the eye as a symbol of God's presence. As the original community who had been catechized for years on the meaning of the eye gradually became less attached to it, the larger community began to search for a new place for the eye of God. The meaningful conversations led to significant new understanding and the bonding of former strangers; the support of new people lessened the grief; and a new mutual understanding of the symbol prompted new thinking about a place for the eye of God.

Continuity: What Is Staying the Same? What Is Changing?

The glue that connects the endings and the new beginnings is like rubber cement. It is flexible. It can easily move one thing from one place to another. Some things that are part of the past may also be part of the future. Certainly things like liturgy, while it may have variations in terms of music and other elements, will be basically the same. The scouting pledges and badges will be same. The work of a combined fire department will have the same essentials. Some practices will continue; some will not. Some will be variations on the original activities.

The questions for conversation during this phase of change are ones similar to the following: What is changing? What is staying the same? What do we want our lives to be like in the future? How will we value our differences? How can we grow together in faith? How can we serve better? What are ways to conserve resources? Who is not here that needs to be part of the conversation? What are the essential elements of our life together? How are we nurturing our imaginations? How are we recognizing and responding to the Spirit within who is helping us yearn for the "more" in our lives? Some things will remain as they have been in the past. The essentials of the organization may remain the same. Perhaps different images and language will be used to proclaim the mission because the community is a new one and will be coming together to continue the conversation about mission, values, and vision.

In one sense, no organization remains the same over time. Change is always happening, though often it is imperceptible. Decisions made during this transition time may be good for the short term, but may need to be revisited over the months and years that follow. Often radical change is implemented in stages. A parish may know it needs to merge with another one and ultimately move into one worship site. However, initially there may be one liturgy a week in both churches, or one church may be used for weddings and funerals. Gradually, as the community becomes more stable and begins to grow, it will be easier to move into the larger, structurally-sound building. Or with a newly merged fire department, each may still serve the same citizens as they did when they were separate, while gradually adapting new software to help them serve the combined region.

If an inner-city nonprofit has been known for ten years for successfully helping low-income people rehab their homes to make them more energy efficient, and the source of funding from the city suddenly dries up, the organization might need to rely more heavily on grants and other sources of funding. It may need to move its offices to conserve resources. It may need to change its procedures. It may need to align itself with Habitat for Humanity or similar organizations. It may need to change its structure. It may go through many transitions, but with adequate funding, its stellar reputation, a comprehensive plan, and bold leadership, it will continue its mission. The mission will not change; its values will not change; but how it does its mission will change based on funding and governmental regulations, etc.

The Future—Hopes and Dreams

The struggles, the endings, the loss, the sense of abandonment—living in the wilderness—are all part of dealing with change and transition. If acknowledged and cared for, the negative parts of living in the wilderness can lead to new hopes, new dreams, new life. Margaret Wheatley notes that work done for the common good does not take away our energy; it pours energy into our bodies through our open hearts and generous spirits. The Prophetic Planning that is supported in this book assumes that while there is pain and loss when something that is cherished is changing or diminishing, there is also good will. Therefore, from the ashes of the old the phoenix will rise, and new energy will be available for creating the future.

Prophetic Planning has led to renewed nonprofits serving people in need with a refreshed vitality; communities being energized to do things they never thought they could do, parishes coming together to form a new congregation, communities of vowed religious realizing all they can do with the "less is more" factor, and local government finding ways to provide services that are less costly.

For Reflection and Discussion

1. Describe a time when you experienced significant change in your life? What was involved? What were the losses? Uncertainties? What was the "wilderness zone" like? What invitations for new beginnings were there?

2. Describe a time when an organization in which you were involved changed significantly. What were the fears? What was lost? What were the new opportunities?

3. What have you learned from dealing with change?

4. What has stayed the same during either personal or organizational changes in your experience?

5. What is one piece of advice you would give someone going through personal or organizational change?

CHAPTER

Conflict Management and Resistance to Change

If we manage conflict constructively, we harness its energy for creativity and development.
KENNETH KAYE*

CONFLICT IS A PROCESS of dealing with differences... Conflict is hard...Conflict is messy...Conflict is as natural as breathing...Conflict can lead to new life and new possibilities.

In earlier chapters, we explored some key dynamics related to both the journey of Prophetic Planning and to change and transition. Regardless of whatever planning process is being implemented or what transition steps are being taken, both realities lead inevitably to certain levels of resistance to change and to conflict. Having a strong commitment to deal effectively with resistance and with conflicts are key ingredients in helping people and organizations grow stronger in the midst of moving forward into the future.

In workshop after workshop on communications, change, and conflict, we are struck by the overly negative response so many people have to words like power, conflict, and change. Many people carry significant

*From *Workplace Wars and How to End Them: Turning Personal Conflicts into Productive Teamwork.* © 1994 Kenneth Kaye.

baggage from their experiences of being participants in meaningful conflicts. When asked to identify a phrase or a feeling associated with conflicts in which they are involved, people say things such as the following:

- I am scared.
- I don't like it.
- I want to run away.
- My stomach gets upset.
- I am afraid I will lose.
- I feel powerless.

Only rarely do we hear, "I am excited," or "There are many positive opportunities in times of conflict." Why do so many respond negatively to conflict and to resistance, and what can we do about it?

First of all, we need to state a few assumptions about the topics at hand.

Assumptions Regarding Conflict

- Conflict and change are facts of life; conflict itself is a neutral reality.
- The fact that people have differences is not the key issue; how we deal or don't deal with them is what matters.
- Conflict is a natural and expected condition.
- All people have value and worth and are worthy of respect.
- Effective communication builds relationships and provides a strong foundation for working together toward a shared mission.
- All conflict is not resolvable, but all conflict can be managed.
- Managing conflict well forms the basis for superior problem solving, creativity, and relationship building.
- Conflict is positive if well-managed, and it is negative if not.

■ In the face of aggressive behavior, passivity invites further aggression, aggressiveness begets more aggression, and assertiveness defuses aggression.

For many people, the assumptions identified above are contrary to their habitual ways of thinking and acting. However, acting on the basis of these assumptions can make an enormous positive difference in the lives of individuals, leaders, groups, and organizations. Two assumptions in particular have a big impact on our work in the midst of conflict—that conflict is a natural and expected condition and that all conflict is not resolvable, but all conflict can be managed.

The first of these two assumptions helps us "plan" various ways of responding to the inevitable conflict situations we face, since they are natural and expected realities. In fact, we often tell our clients that conflict is as natural as breathing. Believing this to be true helps people, even in difficult conflicts, to be more effective since it will be easier to respond rather than react to the other folks involved in the conflict.

The second of these two assumptions is critical, because it helps us establish realistic expectations. Rather than set up the false expectation that all conflicts can be resolved, people are challenged to consider how they can best manage all the conflicts they face, while agreeing to disagree on some and resolving those they can.

Being a Successful Conflict Manager

What are the ingredients to being a successful conflict manager? The first ingredient is to respond well to stress and resistance to change. These realities are often connected, since people are usually under some stress or are experiencing degrees of confusion or anxiety when they are involved in planning for an uncertain future or are experiencing some resistance to the changes ahead as they seek to navigate through times of rapid or major change.

Stress or struggle with planning for the future or with major change or transition is often manifested by increasing levels of resistance to change. For many people, resistance is negative, something to be avoided or ignored or reacted to defensively. We believe it is important to befriend resistance, because it reminds us that something important is going on. This will lessen its impact on plans for the future.

The Five Most Common Reasons Why People Resist Change

According to the Alban Institute, an ecumenical think tank based in Washington, D.C., the five most common reasons people resist change are:

1. A desire to not lose something or someone of value—a personal investment in the present.
2. A misunderstanding of the change and its implications.
3. A belief that the change does not make sense; the "Why?" is not sufficiently answered.
4. A low tolerance for change.
5. A limited trust in those leading the change process.

None of these five reasons is bad. All make good sense given a particular set of circumstances. The challenge for leaders involved in a planning process or dealing with major changes is to keep the levels of resistance at manageable levels—levels where people can still talk with each other and also feel heard by one another.

One way to work effectively in lowering resistance to change or to planning is to view resistance as both an opportunity to receive important feedback and as a resource to consider new perspectives and possibilities. Another effective way to work on lessening resistance in oneself, as well as in others, is to practice deep listening combined with the ability to be genuinely present to others involved in the conflict or change process without judgment or blame.

Principles of Good Communication

The second ingredient to be an effective conflict manager is to practice good communication. Start with listening for the heart of the matter and focusing on what is essential. As one of our mothers often said, "God gave us two ears and one mouth for a reason."

It is important to take responsibility for your own needs, thoughts, and feelings. Rather than speaking in generalities and for other people by saying things like, "All of us believe..." or "We all agree that..." it is better to own your own feelings and thoughts and share them respectfully without blame or judgment.

Being assertive, open, honest, direct, and appropriate in communicating and rejecting aggressive or passive responses builds trusting relationships. As someone once said, "In the face of aggressive behavior, passivity invites aggression and aggressiveness begets aggression, while assertiveness defuses aggression." Another way of talking about these different approaches is to think of assertive communication as the experience of expressing one's wants and needs while respecting the wants and needs of others; whereas aggressive communication means expressing one's wants and needs without respect for the wants and needs of others.

Here are a few elements that make a significant positive difference in managing conflicts successfully:

The Need for Quality Listening

Barriers to more effective listening:

- The listener talks too much.
- The listener doesn't listen for long enough before starting to talk.
- The listener remains silent and entirely unresponsive.

The Need to Pay Attention to Nonverbal Communication

- Eighty percent of all communication is nonverbal—with cultural differences.
- Pay attention to posture, tone of voice, eye contact, space.
- It really is what we do and not what we say that is most important.

The Need to Claim Ownership

- Own your own thoughts and feelings.
- Be proactive and not reactive—choose your responses.
- Check out what you see and hear.

The Need for "I Messages" vs. "You Messages"

- Keep the focus on me **vs.** Put focus on the other.
- Describe my needs **vs.** Seldom mention my needs.
- Describe my feelings **vs.** Seldom mention my feelings.
- Non-judgmental **vs.** Blameful.
- Help build others' self-esteem **vs.** Tend to erode self-esteem.

Have the Courage to Engage in Difficult Conversations

The third ingredient of being an effective conflict manager is challenging to be sure, and usually involves head, heart, and habit. As Stone, Patton, and Heen said in their significant book entitled, *Difficult Conversations: How to Discuss What Matters Most*, every difficult conversation between individuals and groups involves the sorting out of three distinct conversations:

1. The "What happened?" conversation.
2. The feelings conversation.
3. The identity conversation.

This is often easier said than done, because emotions can be running high, resistance can be increasing, and judgment can be in the air. Fortunately, these authors provide a road map to help move through the minefield of significant conflict. They suggest movement toward a learning conversation, and they provide a checklist for difficult conversations.

In order to have a successful learning conversation with individuals or groups in the middle of serious conflict, or to facilitate such conversations, two movements are required:

1. Movement from blame to contribution.
2. Movement from certainty to curiosity.

The movement from blame to contribution is important because instead of playing the blame game ("If only you didn't make that big mistake..." or "It's your fault we are in this mess"), people are encouraged to own the contributions they have made to create "this mess" or to acknowledge perhaps their own mistakes, rather than just the mistakes of others. Once this movement occurs, people are in a much better position to work on positive or win-win outcomes.

In a similar way, the movement from certainty to curiosity helps to also foster win-win outcomes, because the dynamic is no longer that some have certainty ("the answers") and others don't ("the clueless"). Through curiosity and the asking of good questions ("I am curious; why did you act the way you did in that meeting yesterday?" or "I am curious; how can we best work together to problem solve our issues?"), people and groups suddenly find themselves working together and sharing needed information, while also contributing to a satisfactory "both/and" solution rather than to an unsatisfactory "either/or" problem.

All of this effort requires a good deal of courage to act without clearly defined outcomes. It also requires solid levels of confidence and competence to stick with the conflict management initiatives. Stone, Patton, and Heen help with the competence and confidence issues by offering a checklist for these difficult conversations:

■ Prepare by walking through the three types of conversations. (What happened?, feelings, and identity)

■ Check your purposes and decide whether to raise the issue. (What is the hoped for outcome, and will this intervention move us in the right direction?)

■ Start from the third story. (Not my story or your story; not our story or their story; but as the interested observer of both stories. What is the truth in each story that becomes a third story?)

■ Explore their story and yours. (Often moving from the third story to the participants' stories leads to new insight and fresh perspectives.)

■ Problem solving (The opportunity to try and move beyond conflict management to conflict resolution.)

Being Committed to Creative Problem Solving

Creative and effective problem solving requires several essential elements—willing participants, sufficient levels of mutual trust and respect, and at least a mutually agreed-to common or shared outcome. When these elements are in play, a problem-solving approach is worth the effort. Following are a few approaches that can be adapted to specific needs.

One problem-solving approach that helps address real or imagined obstacles is called **STRIDE.** It was first developed by John Scherer and has been adapted by many organizations over the years. The STRIDE approach assumes that a group is working together to solve problems.

S: Real Life Situation

In the situation phase, the problem-solving team comes to a good understanding of the issues involved. The members grasp the impact of the situation on the organization. They become aware of costs associated with the situation. They gain knowledge about who "owns" the situation and begin to look at who is calling for change.

T: Target or Goals

At this stage, the group looks at all possibilities and focuses beyond the problems involved. Establishing targets or even criteria for decision making ensures positive steps toward change. Ultimately constructing goals or "targets to be hit" is the focus of this part of the process for solving the problem.

R: Restraining Forces or Obstacles

Restraining forces refer to opposition to change. This is an analytical stage where determining why the problem continues is important.

I: Ideas or Options

This stage builds on the earlier one. It names possibilities for forward movement. It also calls for brainstorming ways to diminish the restraining forces.

D: Decision(s)

Here the members of the problem-solving team decide what they will do, gain the commitment of the whole problem-solving group, and develop action plans that include who will do what and by when.

E: Evaluation

This phase is accountability-focused. It looks for something measurable to determine how well the decision is being implemented and if the decision is achieving the goals that it was made to accomplish.

Third Party Mediation

A second problem-solving approach includes the recognition that many problems cannot be resolved just by the involved parties. There is in these situations a benefit to having an independent, neutral, third party—a mediator who works with all parties to reach a mutually-desirable outcome. To be effective, a mediator must:

- Be an effective communicator who models deep listening.
- Establish ground rules agreed to by the parties that help promote respectful conversation.
- Identify the issues that must be addressed.
- Facilitate important conversations related to these key issues.
- Help the parties reach agreements they can live with regarding the key issues.
- Be available for additional mediation sessions as the need arises.

Role Reversal

A third approach invites problem solvers to explore the various issues that need to be discussed from the other person's perspective. Rather than get caught up in the "my way or the highway" trap, people are asked to take on the perspective of "the other." To the best of their ability, participants engage in meaningful conversation with others who are open to conflict resolution by taking on the perspective of the individual or group on the "other side." This role reversal often leads to an increase in understanding and respect, as well as to a movement from "my way or your way" to a new "third way." Insights from both perspectives lead to greater wisdom as well as better decisions that can be lived out by all involved parties.

Ministry to Anger

As mentioned earlier, conflicts stir a broad range of emotions as well as thoughts: feelings of anger, sadness, fear, and more. One way of addressing these kind of emotions is through an approach called "Ministry to Anger," developed by Brother Loughlan Sofield, Trinitarian brother and author of the popular book, *Collaborative Ministry: Skills and Guidelines.* This approach recognizes that in any significant circumstance where one or both parties are angry, they can work with their own feelings as well as those of the other party in the following manner:

■ Notice that you and/or the other party are angry.

■ Recognize that anger is often an expression of the experience of being hurt, so ask questions as to if there is hurt and what the hurt is about. The responses to these and related questions will contribute to a deeper understanding of what is taking place.

■ If you want to take this approach further, you can then recognize that hurt is often the result of deeply-held values and beliefs that have been violated. You can ask yourself or the other person, "What are the values and beliefs you hold dear that have been violated and are resulting in the experience of being hurt?"

■ If you want to go further still, you can ask where, how, and why in yours or another's life did you or they come to embrace these particular values and beliefs?

This approach, especially when engaged in openly and honestly by both parties, yields new understanding, greater acceptance of one another (even if serious disagreements remain), and more positive actions by all parties.

The Four Commandments of Contentment

Conflicts can be quite unsettling, so it is also important for people to promote peaceful ways of thinking, feeling and acting as conflicts are managed and resolved. Various meditative practices or ways of slowing down one's breathing as well as movements are quite useful. A particularly beneficial approach involves the "Four Commandments of Contentment." These are:

1. Thou shalt live in the here and now.
2. Thou shalt not hurry.
3. Thou shalt not take thyself too seriously.
4. Thou shalt be grateful.

Practicing these and other steps that help people experience contentment or peace or centeredness make it much more likely that participants in various conflicts can stay in the present moment and succeed in managing and resolving conflicts much more effectively.

Some Closing Perspectives in Managing Conflict Effectively

The insights from this chapter must be connected in the practice of daily living with the related insights from the two previous chapters on Prophetic Planning and on change and transition. The goal of this entire book is to empower readers to move from a theoretical understanding of these themes to a practical way of living them out.

With that in mind, we offer a few additional thoughts:

1. When engaging in conflict management, start with yourself and ask how you are thinking and feeling about the conflict and what you hope for.
2. Consider how you have contributed to the current reality and how others have contributed as well.

3. Begin acting from the heart of the matter and stay focused on what you really want to accomplish.

4. Stop and ask yourself some questions that return you to dialogue:

▪ What do I really want for myself?

▪ What do I really want for others?

▪ What do I really want for the relationship?

▪ How would I behave if I really wanted these results?

5. Take charge of your body.

▪ Our breath is an anchor.

▪ As we introduce complex and abstract questions to our mind, the problem-solving part of our brain recognizes that we are now dealing with intricate social issues and not physical threats.

6. Learn to look for safety problems:

▪ People who are gifted at dialogue keep a constant vigil on safety.

▪ Watch for signs that people are afraid.

▪ Do others feel safe?

▪ When it is safe, you can say anything.

▪ Dialogue calls for the free flow of meaning—period. Nothing kills the flow of meaning like fear.

▪ If you make it safe enough you can talk about most anything and people will listen.

For Reflection and Discussion

1. What does it mean to you to befriend resistance to change?

2. What steps would you take to lower resistance?

3. How would you go about encouraging curiosity when differences emerge in a group?

4. What would you do to foster creative problem solving as part of conflict resolution?

5. What has been your major learning related to conflict management and resistance to change?

CHAPTER

The Role of Faith and Values in the Prophetic Planning Process

The only true voyage of discovery...would be not to visit strange lands but to possess other eyes.
MARCEL PROUST

AN UNDERLYING PREMISE in all successful Prophetic Planning is the belief that human beings are the world's greatest assets. Believing in people's basic good will and trusting that they will work on life's journey toward the common good are foundational to dealing successfully with change. Time after time when working with groups going through significant transitions, we have seen that given an opportunity to help create their future, they have emerged from the change process with more energy for and insight into the future than they had for the present.

People are shareholders of their destiny. They help direct the journey. Through the eyes of faith, they see themselves participating in something much bigger than themselves. From a Judeo-Christian faith perspective, they participate in the reign of God. They share God's life through the covenant of the first Testament, where God calls the Israelites to be God's people, and/or through the Gospels, where people are called to share in the very life of God through

Jesus Christ. When individuals and communities partake in the very life of God, they become shareholders with God in their futures.

Helping people see their lives and challenges through the eyes of faith brings added insights. Using the lens of faith helps people connect the "God of the past" in the present and be energized for the future. In working with Judeo-Christian faith-based groups who see themselves as furthering the reign of God on earth, planning can be guided and inspired by reflecting on the Scriptures and discerning God's call today as the sacred readings are proclaimed. In the Jewish tradition, God is experienced as the "trusted one" who cares and has a personal relationship with the chosen ones. For the Israelites, God is the one who makes promises and fulfills these by being a caring God, a protector, a God who saves the people and guides them. God calls the people to "do justice, and to love kindness, and to walk humbly with your God" (Micah 6:8), thus sharing in the very life of God.

At the heart of humanity is the struggle for the "more" in life. For Christians, Jesus Christ, the Incarnate God, makes God's presence known and proclaims the message of the reign of God. Christ points to "more than meets the eye." In the synoptic Gospels, in Paul's writings and in Acts, it is the merciful love of God which is "the more." It is the identification with the crucified and risen Lord who bestows the Spirit that brings meaning and purpose in life. In this recognition is where the more is found. In John, it is the Word made Flesh where we contemplate the glory of God and discover the more. The more is the intangible mystery of God's presence in human interactions and relationships with all of creation, which generates enthusiasm and joy and sustains during times of loss and difficulty. Recognizing the more is at the heart of planning, especially for faith-based organizations. Teilhard de Chardin, the great Jesuit theologian and paleontologist, reminds us that by reason of creation and the Incarnation, nothing is profane for those who know how to see. It is seeing the more that is at the heart of planning.

Different generations translate what they are looking for in various ways. Some have sought it through the accumulation of material goods, others in military dominance, and others in focusing on activating their human potential. Today's younger generation (eighteen to twenty-nine year olds), described by John Zogby as the first "global generation," are looking for the more in global society consensus-oriented decision making, environmentally sound guidelines, and authenticity from the media, leaders, and institutions. They are also, according to Zogby, looking inward for spiritual comfort. In his 1976 lecture accepting the Nobel Prize in literature, Saul Bellow reminded us that from struggle has come an immense, painful longing for a more comprehensive understanding of the purpose of life and who we are. By connecting change to the "bigger picture," the broader context, and tapping into people's yearnings and beliefs, one is guided to plan so that some of those beliefs may be fulfilled. As planners and shareholders in the reign of God, we are called to be aware of the "bigger picture" and plan with the common good in mind.

Current Reality

Successful planning involves looking at reality and knowing what the current situation is. This involves studying demographics including population trends, income patterns, age spectrums, and educational levels. It also encompasses community needs and financial realities as well as current economics. Understanding the availability of human resources is also at the heart of planning. For instance, if there is a lack of trained dentists for a certain rural area, it is fruitless to build a dental clinic which cannot be staffed. If there are four churches within walking distance of each other and not enough priests to staff them, that needs to be considered in planning for the future. If vowed women religious have always staffed a hospital in a particular community, and they are no longer available, planning must take into consideration how the mission can continue without the leadership of women religious.

Effective change is based on understanding the "world view" of those involved in the transition. Seeing where people are coming from and recognizing how they have been shaped by their experience leads to greater understanding of their struggles. If planners are working with people whose ancestors built churches reflective of their ethnic heritage at great personal sacrifice, it is important to start with an appreciation for the stories of the heroes who constructed the churches. By standing in their shoes with deep reverence for what has been, one discovers a starting point for moving into the future.

Common Good

In the non-faith-based, "not-for-profit" world where reflecting from a religious perspective might not be appropriate, it is still important to place planning in a bigger context before working on a particular focus. Giving attention to how the particular organization contributes to the common good might be a good place to start. Nonprofit organizations typically focus around a health issue (Cancer Society, American Heart Association, Red Cross, etc.) or a social issue (Independence First, Goodwill Industries, various group home associations, etc.). All are related to some aspects of the common good. Reflecting on how the works of the nonprofit contribute to the common good situates them in a larger world and helps planners see similarities between various organizations. This in itself can lead to planning in collaboration with other groups with similar or complimentary purposes. Thinking about the mission of the nonprofit can touch a source of energy and unleash beliefs about oneself, the organization and the purpose of the organization. All planning is enriched by being situated in a larger context than the central mission of the association. Just as planning in faith-based contexts can be located in building the reign of God, so too nonprofit planning can be located in the bigger picture of being shareholders, creating or contributing to the common good.

Faith and Prophetic Planning

In some ways the planning facilitator and those doing the planning take on the role of the prophet. Prophets are people immersed in the life of the community who have a sense of God's promises and guidance. They also have a good "political sense." Those involved in

Prophetic Planning feel called to do this. They have often been tapped on the shoulder as people who are well respected in the community, are faith-filled and open to God's ever-present Spirit. Besides having a sense of being called they have a sense of mission. God has called them at this particular point in time to be about an important aspect of building God's reign on earth. They are called to be shareholders in God's mission. The Prophetic Planner knows when to speak, and like the prophets of old, knows when to be silent. The Hebrew prophets were both concrete in their expressions and consistent in their lifestyles. They put themselves at the service of the community. They did not "foretell" the future as much as they helped prepare the people in the present for the future. They themselves experienced conversion and trusted that their work would ultimately transcend the confines of a particular time and place. They saw themselves as shareholders in God's mission to form a faith-filled community.

John the Baptist was considered a person living the prophetic tradition at the time of Jesus. His role of "preparing the way" is one of the roles Prophetic Planners take on today. The explicit description of him living in the wilderness helps us identify the "wilderness zone" of planning with the prophetic role. His prophetic presence encouraged a sense of hope among people in his time. John the Baptist is an ideal model in some ways for planners today. He was preparing the way as planners do today for what they imagine is a better (maybe more realistic) future. He could manage the "wilderness," the uncertainty of it—the fact that one could not always count on a lot of support in the wilderness. He did not see himself as important, but rather pointed to Jesus as the reason for his existence as a prophet.

Jesus Christ is referred to as "a" prophet (Matthew 21:46) and "the" prophet (John 7:40). Jesus was seen as a prophet in the classical sense of the Israelite prophets. He had a great influence on large crowds of people; people experienced conversion in his presence; be believed in people and gave them the courage to believe not only in a loving God, but also in themselves because of God's love and compassion for them. A prophet is always a mediator, a connector between the present and the future. Jesus was the ultimate mediator between God and humanity, between the reign of God present and the reign to come. Planners are also mediators between what is and what could be in relationship to building the reign of God.

Prophetic Planning, Prayer and Ritual

The oil which keeps the Prophetic Planning process going is prayer and ritual. Through the process of dealing with present realities, diminishing resources, loss, grief, new hopes, and ultimately new realities, prayer and ritual ground the Prophetic Planning process in something deeper than itself. They connect the community to the gracious God, who is bringing them forth to be a new community. Unpacking the meaning of the Scriptures, reflecting on the lives of those who have gone before us, blessing with water, nurturing through liturgy, anointing with oil, lighting candles to remind us of the presence of the Spirit, raising incense—all keep us grounded in what is really important to us and remind us that we are not engaged in Prophetic Planning alone.

Ritual is particularly important in the change process. Ritual is an essential ingredient in human development and is necessary both for individual growth and communal maturity. The experience of ritual helps bond the community and gives it a sense of the sacred which words alone cannot always accomplish. Ritual is an activity which is repetitive, interpersonal, and value based. Rituals are full of many levels of meaning. Lighting a candle brings new light to a room. Lighting a candle in a prayer context reminds people of the presence of the Spirit. Lighting a candle and placing it next to an enthroned Bible helps the community be aware of the power of the Word of God. When God speaks, something happens. In a prayerful context, the community realizes that God is speaking as the Word is proclaimed.

Reflection and ritual are also important for non-faith-based groups engaged in Prophetic Planning. Reflection on the meaning and purpose of the life of the group, accompanied by either a water ritual or a light one, can contribute to the bonding of those gathered, as well as point to deeper realities of the group's existence and mission.

What Prophets Contribute to the Planning Process

Prophets consistently reminded people of what God had done for them in the past. They referred to God's creation, covenants, compassion, mercy, love, and tenderness, and demand that people be the best they can be for the sake of others, the covenant, and ultimately the reign of God on earth. The Prophetic Planning process is rooted in remembering the past and the values inherent in the past. It cherishes stories from the past, and listens and celebrates them with reverence.

Prophets are always calling people to conversion, a change of heart, greater faithfulness to God's promises, seeing life with the eyes of faith, reaching out to others with healing balm. Prophetic Planning is not a straight line from current reality to the preferred future reality. It is navigating a wilderness zone where people are called to let go of some of the comforts of the past, embrace those who are hurting, name the losses, and gradually take a few steps forward. We must ecognize that there will be a few taken back as progress is made by taking a few steps forward and a few backward until one is "out of the wilderness."

Jesus was a bold prophet. He challenged the *status quo.* "Now you Pharisees clean the outside of the cup and of the dish, but inside you are full of greed and wickedness. You fools! Did not the one who made the outside make the inside also?" (Luke 11:39–40). He spoke of what was really important and did not focus on the small stuff: " 'You shall love the Lord your God with all your heart, and with all your soul, and with all your mind, and with all your strength.' The second is this, 'You shall love your neighbour as yourself.' There is no other commandment greater than these" (Mark 12:30–31). He set the bar high: "Be perfect, therefore, as your heavenly Father is perfect" (Matthew 5:48). Prophetic planners, as shareholders in God's world, are called to be bold, to take risks, to set high standards.

Jesus was always discerning God's spirit in his life and helped his disciples to do the same. He felt the need for prayer and would often get up early to pray, to discern God's will (see Mark 1:35). He gave precise instructions to his disciples to go out and preach and discern whether they were welcome or not (see Luke 10:1–12). He prayed that he might not have to die, but surrendered to the will of God (see Luke 22:42).

While many recognized prophets operated out of and worked explicitly in a religious environment, others operated primarily in the political or civic arena. Ghandi, Martin Luther King, Jr., the founders of Doctors Without Borders, etc., just to name a few, worked primarily in a social realm beyond the boundaries of a specific religion. They were faith-filled people formed by a spirituality marked by peace and justice. Every organization that serves the needs of others has prophets who have contributed to its initiatives. Getting in touch with the faith and convictions of those heroes and heroines can provide insights and motivation for a successful planning process.

What do Prophets and Planners Have in Common?

Prophetic Planning calls for planners to be people who:

- Are shareholders in God's life, mission, and vision for the world.
- See life through the lens of faith and focus on the "more" in life, whether in a religious sphere or in a secular one.
- Are in touch with and appreciate the rich history of the past.
- Reflect on God's presence and are open to the Spirit.
- Courageously speak up for what is right.
- Understand the current reality.
- Have the ability to steer a course through the "wilderness."
- Have an inclusive and large worldview with an eye toward the common good.
- Can inspire people to change and help sustain them on the way.
- Recognize the value of ritual and storytelling.
- Are patient with and in touch with the "slow work of God."

The Articulation of Values in Prophetic Planning

Values are often implicit in planning. As noted above, they are celebrated through ritual. Values are the underlying principles upon which thrusts are taken and decisions are made. Values reflect core beliefs. Some of the values which permeated the stories of the biblical prophets included:

■ Trust in the presence of God and that God trusted them to do prophetic work to which they were called.

■ Faith that they could make a significant difference in the life of the community.

■ Courage to speak in the name of God.

■ Perseverance in fulfilling their call from God.

■ Patience in knowing that change happens slowly.

■ A propensity to listen to the soft whispers of God's voice in the community.

When working with planning groups, it is important to help them articulate their values. Values are guiding principles of conduct by which an organization lives. Arriving at the expression of them often galvanizes organizations to come to a deeper understanding of who they are. For it is in understanding their purpose and identity and their core beliefs that they are empowered to envision their future.

Example #1: Values in an Organization Dedicated to the Healing Ministry

One organization whose primary purpose is to be part of the healing ministry of a Christian church included the following values in its planning efforts:

■ Integrity—living out moral and ethical principles.

■ Service—caring for those in need with generosity and hospitality.

■ Compassion—responding to the call of Jesus by sharing the suffering, hope, and joy of others.

■ Inclusivity—welcoming, honoring, and fostering diversity that leads to unity.

■ Leadership—being credible and prophetic with those we serve, our members, and our profession.

■ Empowerment—encouraging others to use their gifts within and beyond their profession.

The process of discerning these values energized the organization to think "bigger" than what they currently imagined as their mission and ministry. Those involved in the planning saw themselves as shareholders in something broader than themselves.

Example 2: Values in a Catholic School

A faith-based elementary school, through their planning process which included staff and parents, spoke of their values in the following way:

Values espoused by school (name):

■ Focus on the whole child—fostering the spiritual, emotional, intellectual, social, and physical development of our children, while recognizing each one's uniqueness.

■ Academic excellence—measuring our programs, teachers, and students against the highest national standards.

■ Faith—embodying the practice of family values and participation in the life the Church.

■ Respect—reflecting human dignity in our actions toward self and others.

■ Responsibility—being accountable for one's actions and attitudes.

■ Reverence—demonstrating honor for God and all God's creatures.

■ Diversity—exemplifying our commitment to attract students and faculty who represent the cultural, economic, and family makeup of our community.

These values, particularly the one on diversity, raised awareness of the racial diversity in the community and the desire to be more inclusive in its outreach. The consensus around the diversity value was not accomplished without some controversy. Ultimately, despite some dissenting voices, there was consent that these indeed were the values of the school. The process of discerning values can of itself bring about a change in attitude and actions for given groups. In this case, the prophetic inclusion of a diversity value enabled the school community to be more aware of the larger community and its mission to embrace differences for the good of all its students and their families.

Example 3: Values in a Parish

As parishes engage in planning for the future, they too find it enriching to begin to articulate their values. In so doing, they come to a deeper understanding of who they are and what their core beliefs are. In one particular instance, they articulated them as:

We value…

■ Celebrating who we are as a faith community through liturgy, sacraments, and prayer.

■ Being an accepting, welcoming, and evangelizing community in our actions and attitudes toward all.

■ Being a learning community committed to lifelong Catholic faith formation and to passing on the faith to the next generation.

■ Respecting the life and dignity of all and working for justice in the world.

■ Serving the spiritual, emotional, and physical needs of others through outreach opportunities, including our sister parish in Peru.

■ Being good stewards of God's gifts.

The utterance of these values helped the parish shape its ministerial efforts. They were not just words on paper, but direction setting beliefs which needed to be enfleshed by the actions of the community.

Example 4: Values in a Nonprofit Adult Learning Organization

All organizations operate out of values, spoken or unspoken. One urban nonprofit adult learning organization, which serves under-educated adults, enhanced its own self-awareness by discovering its underlying values or core beliefs. They then were able to use these to secure funding from grantors who supported the values. They stated their values as:

We believe...

- Education is a fundamental right.
- All people are entitled to equal educational opportunities.
- Mutual respect is essential to our mission.
- Each person is unique and has worth and dignity.
- The whole person deserves development through education in a safe and supportive environment.
- The adult learning center benefits all who participate in and contribute to its mission—staff, volunteers, students, and donors.

One of the great insights this group got from struggling to succinctly speak its values was the renewed understanding that everyone involved at the center benefits, not just the students.

Faith and Values in Prophetic Planning

The four hallmarks of Prophetic Planning—respecting the past, embracing conversion, being bold, and discerning God's will—are rooted in faith. Faith draws on the resources of the biblical tradition. It possesses the courage of the prophetic practice and reflects the simplicity of God and God's actions in and through the community. Faith embraces the stories of the past, the ritual celebrations which reinforce the community's awareness of the presence of God and response to it, as well as the values inherent in and inseparable from humanity's relationship with God. Faith makes people shareholders in God's reign in the world.

Prophetic Planning unleashes faith as it is articulated in the values espoused by organizations. These core beliefs flow out of the more fundamental belief in God's saving presence and humanity's response to it in contributing to the reign of God on earth.

Given this, for planning to be truly prophetic it needs to:

■ Call people forward to exercise their prophetic role in the life of their organization.

■ Provide opportunities and resources to deepen one's faith through prayer, reflection on Scripture, and the intersection of culture and faith.

■ Offer opportunities to articulate the group's values, based on its purpose and core beliefs.

■ Present processes for understanding the current reality, imagining a preferred future, and moving toward creating a sustainable future as shareholders in the reign of God and the common good of humanity.

■ Give support and leadership for the times the group is in the "wilderness zone."

■ Celebrate through story and ritual what has been and what will be.

Faith and values underlie all successful Prophetic Planning. They bring a sense of meaning and purpose to the planning process. The acknowledgement that a group is planning in some way to enhance the common good or build the reign of God gives it a reason to begin what may turn out to be a difficult process. Naming the values out of which one is living empowers groups to be creative and to have a sense of purpose. They become proud of who they are and who they wish to become.

For Reflection and Discussion

1. To what degree does faith play a role in your organization?
2. How would you describe the faith upon which your organization is built?
3. How does your organization's planning process include ways to discover the big picture?
4. In what ways have you structured prayer or reflection and ritual into your planning processes?
5. What values does your organization espouse?

CHAPTER

Envisioning the Future

The best way to take care of the future is to take care of the present moment.

THICH NHAT HANH

AS WE JOURNEY THROUGH LIFE, these important words remind us both as individuals and organizations that the future grows out of the present moment. Indeed, the future that results from the Prophetic Planning process also must be connected with the past to ensure a meaningful continuity in the midst of genuine change.

Creative, effective, and dynamic planning processes help organizations move from the present into a new future when planning is not viewed as an end in itself but rather as a means to an end—more focused and faithful, with practical action. The future must be prepared for, worked for, even created by leaders and many others committed to a particular organization and its past, present, and future. Truly renewing an organization or helping to create a new future requires the ability to imagine a new and preferred future, while overcoming present obstacles.

In this chapter, we will explore a number of ways that planning processes can assist leaders and organizations to prepare for, envision, and move confidently into the future.

Being able to envision the future helps individuals and organizations journey through the wilderness, letting go of the losses and starting to see the new beginnings. This requires a disciplined effort with significant participation by many throughout the organization. Engaging the minds and hearts of many shareholders in an organization is critical. The more people are involved in the process, the more they will be committed to the outcome. We will address several approaches to envisioning the future of an organization—through goals, objectives, and action steps—and through three different visioning activities. Lastly, we will take a birdseye view of two different images, one a bridge and the other a loop, which can be used to envision Prophetic Planning from a broad perspective.

Goals, Objectives, and Action Steps

Goals are specific points that an organization seeks to attain. A vision usually represents the achievement of multiple goals, while goals are typically stepping stones toward a vision. Goals are also considered "centers of energy" and are long term in nature. They do not usually change during a planning cycle. Some sample goals from a faith-based and nonprofit organization that provide both direction and a glimpse of the hoped for future include:

For a Parish or Congregation

- To celebrate God's presence in word and sacrament.
- To build a welcoming and inclusive faith community for all.
- To nurture, strengthen, and empower the family.
- To promote lifelong faith formation and spiritual development.
- To support our youth and young adults as active members of the community.
- To foster stewardship as a way of life.
- To call all to serve the needs of our time on behalf of peace and justice.

■ To strengthen collaboration, communication, and cooperation among all leaders throughout the parish.

■ To manage all human, financial, technology, and facility resources with responsibility, trust, and accountability.

For a Nonprofit Organization

■ To develop and enhance programs and resources for residents.

■ To be a leader in providing residential support services for people with developmental disabilities.

■ To support and retain quality, specialized employees.

■ To strengthen community relationships and financial support.

■ To be good stewards of agency, financial, and facility resources.

The achievement of multiple goals leads to the realization of an organization's vision, which we will discuss later in this chapter.

Objectives and action steps answer the question, "What will we need to do in the short term so that we can achieve our goals?" In this sense, action steps are the means to achieve the ends which are the objectives, while objectives are the means to achieve the ends which are the goals. To be useful, therefore, objectives must specify goals and action steps needed to be **SMART**:

■ **S**pecific

■ **M**easurable

■ **A**chievable

■ **R**esponsibilities identified

■ **T**ime-bound

The process of identifying an action plan includes specific action steps with measurables, financial implications, and the people responsible for implementation. This approach reflects the insight of futurist Joel Barker, who has commented that vision and action separately do very little, but vision married with action can change the world.

Visioning Activities

It is wise to begin with a focus on imagining the desired or preferred future before addressing obstacles to the future. There are many ways to envision the future. Three approaches follow:

- A visioning activity
- A "magic carpet ride"
- Scenario planning

The Last Five Years

This visioning activity invites planning leaders to be bold and to tune into their hopes and dreams. The first step uses imagination and involves placing oneself "five years from now" into the future. The second step is a writing activity that begins with these words: "The last five years for our organization have been great and graced because…" Once everyone on the planning team has completed at least five to ten "becauses," the third step begins. People are invited to share their ideas one at a time around the circle until all ideas have been shared. Applause is encouraged after each idea is revealed to keep spirits high and to thank everyone for the gifts being shared. The fourth step includes a synthesizing of ideas according to themes. The fifth step welcomes a serious conversation from the planning group about the merits of what has been identified. Finally, a writing group is selected to craft one or two draft vision statements for further review.

The Magic Carpet Ride

The "magic carpet ride" is another type of activity that makes effective use of our imaginations and helps planners to chart the future. The facilitator invites participants to close their eyes, climb aboard the magic carpet, and travel through time and space to consider the past, present, and future of an organization. The magic carpet can also help participants "visit," through their imaginations, the internal and external strengths and weaknesses—as well as threats and opportunities—facing the organization right here and right now. The result of the magic carpet ride can then be summarized in words and images and provide elements that will lead to a new organizational vision.

Scenario Planning

Scenario planning involves a three step process to help organizations move forward. These steps include:

1. Possible futures (identified through a brainstorming activity where "every idea is a good idea").
2. Probable futures (identified after analyzing the pros and cons of the possible futures).
3. Preferred future (identified after reflection, prayer, and discernment).

What is exciting about scenario planning is what happens when people are encouraged to dream big dreams through the brainstorming activity and are then invited to use their analytical skills in moving the process from the possible to the probable futures. There is often a real synergy of ideas and an abundance of future options for individuals and groups to consider. The whole most often is much greater than the sum of the parts.

In scenario-building, different circumstances are imagined for the future. To build scenarios, key factors need to be identified. Driving forces have got to be recognized. Uncertainties must be acknowledged. For instance, if a community is planning an addition for their local school and that addition is dependent upon making fundraising goals, Prophetic Planning requires that different scenarios be developed depending on the timing of the building completion. Some scenarios include:

■ **Scenario 1:** If we reach our goal of $6,000,000 by August 2011, our addition on our school will be finished for August 2012 in enough time to accommodate our anticipated higher enrollment.

■ **Scenario 2:** If we do not reach out goal, we will need to rent portable trailers for classrooms to accommodate the enrollment.

■ **Scenario 3:** If we do not rent temporary trailers for classrooms, we will have to have waiting lists for kindergarten and first grade.

■ **Scenario 4:** If we do not rent trailers for classrooms, we will use the multipurpose and band room for forty students per room and hire teachers' aids full time.

Each of these scenarios has its strengths and concerns. Any one scenario may be totally unacceptable. For instance, in an area where tornados are prevalent, trailers as temporary classrooms may be out of the question for safety reasons. Or having waiting lists may not be acceptable as the enrollment will diminish when the new addition is completed. Scenarios need to be studied. Their assumptions need to be understood and tested. Conversations need to occur about the positive aspects of each scenario, as well as any concerns related to implementing each one. After a thorough analysis and many well-framed conversations among shareholders, a decision needs to be made based on various contingencies about which scenario will be implemented and under what conditions.

Bridging the Future

After years of planning work in the Archdiocese of Milwaukee, Noreen Welte developed the following paradigm to help organizations plan for the future. In this picture, a plan is seen as a bridge from a "foggy" or confused present reality to a clear and affirmed future reality or "best case scenario."

What Does Organizational Planning Look Like?

Organizational planning is a process that:

■ Seeks wisdom from "imple-
menters" and shareholders
in the design of the process.

Focus on the plan.

■ Identifies mission, values, and
vision for vital congregations
and parishes.

Envision the plan.

■ Reviews specific issues of
staffing, relationships,
financing, and programs.

See the plan for what it is now.

■ Considers "best case scenarios"
in light of stewardship and
high quality.

See the plan for what it could be.

■ Builds SMART action steps
to achieve the best case
scenario over time.

Build the plan.

■ Builds successful
implementation teams.

Work the plan.

■ Keeps tabs on progress;
evaluates and updates
over time.

Evaluate/update the plan.

A Planning Loop: What Are the Four Key Stages in the Planning Process?

The following graphic is based on the work of Father George Wilson, SJ, from Management Design Inc., based in Cincinnati, Ohio. It breaks out a traditional planning process into four key stages. These build on the shared experiences and dreams of the founding individuals and groups and can be summarized as follows:

1. Directional planning (mission, value, and vision statements).
2. Strategic planning (goals and priorities and issues).
3. Operational planning (objectives and action steps).
4. Administrative planning (monitoring and evaluating).

Successful planning for an organization requires a focus on the first three areas outlined above in order to facilitate constructive action. What follows are brief descriptions of these elements.

Directional Planning

Mission statement: Why does the organization exist? What is its identity and purpose? What makes the organization unique or distinctive?

Value statements: These statements reflect the core values or key beliefs of the organization. They provide guiding principles of conduct and name what an organization is willing to stand up for. Values are often implicit within organizations, but are most helpful when made explicit. Values are important for a planning process because they help measure the correctness of a given plan. Will living out these values help us live out our mission and live into our vision?

Vision statement: What will the organization look like once its mission is fully realized? This is a longer statement, usually more poetic, and written in the present tense as if the vision has been accomplished. This statement expresses the hoped for results of living out a mission.

Strategic Planning

Goal Statements: These statements are specific points that the organization seeks to attain. A vision usually represents the achievement of multiple goals, while goals are typically stepping stones toward a vision. Goals are long term in nature and do not usually change.

Issues: An effective planning process must help an organization deal with key issues that challenge an organization in the present and will impact the future. These issues are usually both internal and external. There can be many such issues, but some typical issues relate to staffing, funding, facilities, and relationships.

Operational Planning

Objectives: These statements answer the question, "What will the organization need to do in order to achieve its goals?" Objectives break down goals into manageable parts.

Action steps: Action steps make goals operational and measurable. To be useful, action steps need to be **SMART**: Specific, Measurable, Achievable, Responsibilities identified, Time-bound.

Administrative Implementation

Day-to-day monitoring of activities: Administrators use the plan strategically in their everyday activities. Performance is measured by implementation of action steps.

Evaluation: Administrators provide evaluations, usually to boards that monitor the plan and make needed adjustments.

THE REID GROUP
Organizational Planning Cycle

Programs **Issues**	**Objectives**
STRATEGIC	OPERATIONAL
Goals **Priorities**	**Action Steps**
DIRECTIONAL	ADMINISTRATIVE
Mission **Values** **Vision**	**Day-to-Day Activities** **Monitoring Activities** **Evaluation**

Shared Dreams
Shared History
Shared Experiences

Adapted from MDI (Management Design Institute).

This chapter presented various phases of planning processes which can be used in Prophetic Planning. The future can be envisioned through a process of designing goals, objectives, and action steps. It can be designed by visioning activities such as imagining what the situation will look like five years from now if our best hopes and dreams come true. It can be imagined through a "magic carpet trip" or scenario planning. Two images of an overall planning process congruent with the principles of Prophetic Planning were also briefly described. They are incorporated into models presented in Chapter Seven.

For Reflection and Discussion

1. What energizes you when you think about the future of your organization?

2. What concerns you when you consider the future?

3. What role does imagination play when it comes to planning for the future?

4. If you could remove all the obstacles, what would your organization look like a year from now?

5. Name the assets that your organization needs to build upon as it prepares for the future.

CHAPTER **6**

Dealing With Grief and Loss

Organizational Grieving is working through the question: "Who are we now and what does our life together as a group really mean without the vision of our prior selves as a group?

J. GORDON MYERS*

CHANGE BRINGS ABOUT LOSS and loss brings about change. No matter which is the starting point, loss and grief are part of the human experience. Grieving is a process of adjusting to loss. Individuals grieve the loss of spouses, children, parents, and friends through death. People suffer when they lose a job or a home through a house fire, or a valued item they have misplaced. Loss is an emptiness that is painful as well as full of potential. In terms of the paschal mystery, it was through the death of one person, Jesus Christ, that new life came into the world. In the loss of something precious and cherished, the seeds of new life emerged. Many of the ideas in this chapter originated from J. Gordon Myers and have been adapted to encompass many kinds of change, grief, and loss. The chart on page 64, which was introduced in Chapter Two, focuses on the "Endings" and the "Hurts" ("Losses, Scars and Things to Let Go Of"), as well as what will remain the same.

*From *People & Change: Planning for Action.* © 1998 Oriel Incorporated. All rights reserved.

Transition Process

Grief is not only an experience of individuals; it is an occurrence in organizations. Groups also grieve. Grief is a deeply mysterious process that involves sorrow, confusion, and often anger. Both individuals and groups are called throughout their lives to work through a process of knowing what it is they are letting go of (even though it is good and grace-filled) and what the group is holding onto and brings into the future. One of the works of the wilderness zone is to deal with loss and grief.

When organizations merge or consolidate, there are many losses. Offices may relocate; buildings may not be used; procedures may not be the same; roles and responsibilities may change; ways of doing things may not continue. Things will not be the same or feel the same. "Endings" are very public. They are visible. Headquarters may move to a different city. The CEOs may change. Churches used for worship for over a hundred years may not be used in the future. Schools may combine to use one building instead of three. Names of organizations may not be the same.

While endings are very public, losses are private. Losses result from something ending. They are often hidden but poignantly felt. In the change process, one might experience a loss of security. ("Where will I sit? Where will I park? Who will I know?") The pride in belonging to a certain group in a parish may be lost. The satisfaction of knowing your efforts counted and you made a difference may no longer be felt. A sense of joy and contentment may be difficult to achieve. The identity that was unique to your organization or parish may have disappeared with the merged organization.

Understanding the process in the wilderness zone of dealing with grief and loss in a healthy way will empower newly formed organizations to begin their new existence on healthy ground. Avoiding "win-lose" situations is at the heart of successful change. By allowing and acknowledging some resistance to change, the organization can learn from it and open new doors to greater adaptation to fresh ways of being together. It is also a way to ensure that the new community will be formed on a "valued past."

Signs of Grieving

On an individual level, grieving is often characterized initially by numbness or panic. When a spouse dies, the living spouse may get through the wake and funeral with a sense of numbness. Later on, panic may set in, especially related to tasks the spouse did which the survivor may not know how to do. Later on, it may be nostalgia and protest, followed by discouragement and disorientation. Months after a death, a little thing like attending a wedding alone may present new grieving and loss challenges.

Numbness and Panic

Groups go through similar processes of grieving. They may vacillate between numbness and panic. If the change involves consolidating a parish, the numbness may sound like: "I can't imagine not celebrating St. Patrick's Day the way we have been doing it for the last seventy years," or "Mary Sue always wanted to be married in this church. Where will she go now?" If a men's and women's YW/MCA decides to merge and use one set of buildings, numbness might sound like: "Where will they do the tot swimming classes, when all they have is the big Olympic pool?" "What will happen to all our women's groups?" "Will they have to be co-ed?" "Where will we ever go for breakfast after aerobics? There is nothing around there that is open." These kinds of puzzling questions point to the confusion brought about by change.

Nostalgia and Protests

The second phase of corporate grief is nostalgia and protest. People often fluctuate between longing for the past and protesting the anticipated future. Memories of the "good old days" are often tainted with anger and some hostility. In faith-based organizations such as parishes or congregations, nostalgia and protests can be extremely painful because of the assumption that "faith" does not change. Everything around people may be changing, but the one thing they thought they could count on is church being the same. The thought of the comfort of one's parish changing is often beyond imagination. The pain, especially in ethnic communities where the group's ancestors may have made huge sacrifices to build marvelous edifices reflecting the faith, is often very poignant. Often, as ethnic groups in the second and third generation become more assimilated in a less distinguishing American culture, the fear of losing ethnic identity is striking. The closing of an ethnic church becomes a larger symbol of what is feared to be the diminishment of a particular culture.

Some of the same nostalgia can also be present when organizations change offices. When a smaller department or organization is asked to leave their cozy quarters where they all had lunch around a kitchen table and join either another or the larger organization where everyone eats in the cafeteria, something is lost. It is often the family feeling, the more intimate feeling of sharing one another's lives and the sense of a team working together. The same losses are felt when two small town fire or police departments merge into one. Wherever the main office is, that town is perceived to be "the winner," and the other department the "loser."

Discouragement and Disorientation

The third phase of dealing with grief and loss is the tension between discouragement and disorientation. To some it will appear as if it is useless to begin again. So much has been lost that there is little energy to start all over again. At other times it will appear that the group does not even know where to begin. The corporation is confused about the starting points. Where does the old end and the new begin? What can be saved from the old? Who can take the lead? Who wants to do any of this? These questions describe many of the feelings at this stage of dealing with grief and loss.

How to Move Forward

Five strategies can help groups move forward from the unsettledness of dealing with endings and losses. The first is an invitation to participate in the formation of the "new." Timing for this request is important. People need to acknowledge their own pain and loss and have others recognize it before they can move forward. Announcing changes, followed by an immediate invite to be part of the new, is often ineffective. Inviting people to participate in the change-making—giving them time to share their loss and remember their past—is a more appropriate way to enable people to move forward.

The second element in helping people have energy to move forward is to constantly communicate with them. Communication cannot be overdone. Saying the same thing in different ways and in different media can ease some of the tensions. Explaining the "why" of the tensions and the normalcy of them is also appropriate. If people know that their negative feelings are to be expected, that feeling upset is normal, they tend to let go more easily than if their feelings are disregarded or ignored.

The third strategy in helping people resolve some of their destabilization is to provide them with educational opportunities. Make sure they know the demographic realities, including financial ones. Lead them to see the positive elements of the change. Point out how the change will ensure a brighter future. Guide those experiencing change to imagine a well-working organization that can be identified as serving the community well.

The fourth strategy, which can be incorporated into all of the others or seen separately from them, is to provide opportunities for storytelling and ritualizing both the old—what has served well in the past—and the hopes and dreams for the future. This strategy will be further explored in a later section of this chapter.

The fifth strategy is to give the shareholders opportunities to realize what is not changing. To be able to see what is staying the same and to name it enables people to ultimately begin to create the new based on what is not changing. It helps re-orient people to what is really essential to their community or organization. Questions to ask to help people get in touch with what is not changing include the following:

1. What will still be the same when the anticipated change happens?

2. In a faith context, what beliefs have not changed? What rituals are unchanging in their essence? What has deepened through the journey in the wilderness?

3. In a faith context, in what ways has God's presence remained the same? Become more apparent? When did it seem a little "cloudy"?

4. In a nonprofit setting, what core values are still part of our new reality?

Role of Change Leadership

The goal of leadership in times of change is to help groups move from disorientation to meaningful future. Radical change often leads to a loss of meaning. The death of a spouse can bring with it a loss of meaning or purpose. The identity of the person is "halved." Life is not the same with the loss of the significant other.

When there is significant change in groups, meaning is often lost or altered. When the American Heart Association moved to a centralized position from many locally led chapters loosely tied together, there was a loss of a particular pride and ownership for the fine work the local chapter was doing. There was less motivation. Power had been taken away. They no longer had the control they had in the past.

When there is radical change in faith-based organizations such as parochial schools or parishes, especially if it calls for merging or regionalizing schools or parishes, there is often a sense of loss of meaning, lack of power, and isolation. There may be a sense of alienation from those who "caused" the change. The role of the leader is to help the group transition from a loss of meaning to a new sense of purpose, from a lack of power to a degree of control, from isolation to involvement, and ultimately, from disorientation to a greater consciousness of what is not changing—from alienation to community.

Processes Related to Moving From Endings to New Beginnings

No group dealing with change can rush through the wilderness zone. No two groups move from disorientation to new beginnings at the same rate of speed. No two groups have the exact same issues they need to resolve before they can move forward. That being said, there are processes for going through the wilderness that are healthy and life-giving. Some are outlined below.

1. Remembering through storytelling: We are a people of story. As shareholders in the reign of God, we tell stories not only to remember the past, but to make the values and narrative come alive today. Story connects us to who we are and who we are called to be. As communities of vowed religious, parishes, congregations, and corporations come together organizationally or for certain

works, they need to set aside time for storytelling. Remembering the "oldest" story told in the community, the funniest story, the most tragic story, and so on are ways of sharing culture, the past, and hopes for the future. Sharing stories for other groups to hear begins to bond separate communities into one.

2. Seeing what is lost: Stories help us to see what has been lost. When told well, stories of the past engage the listener in the culture of those telling the story. They make come alive what the storyteller is proud of. They connect the listeners to what is/was best in the past. Stories told of and by cherished communities are touching, informative, humorous, and life-giving. Stories can also point to what is staying the same, which will help re-root the shareholders in some core beliefs.

3. Naming what is lost: Listening to the stories and appreciating them, telling stories, and recalling stories are part of reverencing the past. Interpreting the meaning in the stories and naming the losses helps bond strangers, diminishes alienation, and begins to form community. Taking the time to unpack the stories is essential. Stories are not meant to entertain, but to unite people who do not know each other very well and to heal the wounds of misunderstanding, betrayal, and confusion. Naming essential beliefs inherent in the stories also helps people connect to the source of their faith.

4. Acting upon what is named: As stories begin to unfold, the beliefs and values of the communities begin to become clearer to the strangers. Listening to each community's stories helps everyone see the strengths of each community, what they do well, how they could work together. By processing the stories, energy is released from what were formerly isolated groups. They begin to discern key ideas about a common purpose and partnership, which can connect the disparate groups.

5. Connecting story memories to scriptural stories for faith-based groups has the added advantage of linking people to their spiritual roots by relating the current stories with the lives of the biblical

heroes and heroines. This connection reduces the sense of isolation. If the revered characters from the Scriptures suffered similar losses to what people are experiencing today, there is a certain synergy that happens in the realization of the resemblances. The comparison frees groups from some of the bondage of grieving.

Rituals Have Healing Power and an Energizing Potential

Using storytelling in combination with rituals has a powerful impact on groups. People raised in the Christian tradition, especially the Roman Catholic tradition, have access to the power of ritual in the sacramental structure of prayer and worship. Because of these experiences, they may be more comfortable using light, water, oil, bread, and wine in ritual celebrations, apart from sacraments.

Powerful rituals, however, also can be celebrated in non-religious environments with the result of deepening the group's experience of whatever is the focus of the ritual. For instance, using candles to symbolize lighting the way through a dark time or place can be an influential and insightful experience for any group going through a difficult time or a time of uncertainty.

Images can be the basis of rituals. According to Gail Ramshaw in *Treasures Old and New,* "images are bowls filled with meaning." In a situation where two or three parishes are consolidating to form one new parish, a simple ritual to use with storytelling involves inviting parishioners from each of the two or three parishes to come to an evening of storytelling and ritual and to bring a bowl. Have three to five people from each parish come prepared to tell an important story from their parish. Set a time limit of not more than five minutes per story.

Begin with an opening prayer and a story from the Scriptures, with a time for reflection and sharing. Invite each storyteller to share his or her story. Between each story, have questions for discussion such as: What did I learn about the parish from that story? What did I learn that parish is proud of from that story? What strength of the parish shined forth in that story? Share the reflections in small groups. At the end of the time together, provide each person with a lit votive candle (in a holder). Invite each person to share in a thanksgiving prayer for the light which a parish, other than their own, brings to the new consolidation. Example: "I pray in gratitude for St. Gertrude's strong catechetical program. Let us pray to the Lord." All respond: "Lord, hear our prayer." Invite members of each parish to bring their candles forward to a pre-arranged setting around a Bible. After all have done this, note what a strong light the newly merged parish will be to the community. Close with singing a hymn which all know.

The ritual could also be done with other kinds of candles. One larger candle is lit after each story. A votive candle is lit by each group as they discuss the questions and share a "headline" in the large group. The gradual increase of light in the room after each story is told speaks to the gifts of each group or parish. The ritual speaks for itself. It does not need a lot of explanation. It has the power to bond a community and to begin to heal some of the pains of loss and abandonment. Rituals using water (symbolizing new life) or oil (representing the strength needed for the journey), along with Scripture, have not only the power to heal, but also to energize and transform segmentation into a new whole—to transform small isolated groups into a unified community. But it will not happen overnight. Being patient, committed, and creative are needed during this poignant time in the wilderness zone.

For an excellent narrative with practical examples on the role of ritual in parish closures, please see *A Struggle for Holy Ground* by Michael Weldon, OFM. His focus on forgiveness and reconciliation is helpful, especially in situations where a lot of anger has been generated.

The principal tasks involved in walking with people through the wilderness zone involve four primary responsibilities:

1. Help people regain trust and feel included in a situation where they feel isolated. Allowing for anger and negativity to be vented,

managing it, publically acknowledging it, and guiding some exploration of it will normally lead to some letting go and gradual acceptance of the change. Not doing these things will further entrench negative attitudes and keep people captivated by their pain.

2. Invite people to get organized around their future to show them that they do have power and influence. Having them imagine a preferred future helps build their confidence and flexibility. They will begin to take small steps if they get some assurances that they can be successful and that they are not alone.

3. Promote cooperation and sharing, not only of stories, but also of resources to begin helping people move from feeling isolated to seeing that they can be part of a larger team where differences are valued. Providing opportunities for prayer, storytelling, and ritual is a way of walking with those suffering loss and experiencing great change. Rituals heal the community when it is most vulnerable.

4. Lead with patience and example to help people articulate what is staying the same amidst the change. Change will not be seen as an enemy, but rather as an ally, as people bond to a greater degree and cherish the basic elements of the faith or the basic mission of the organization that is not changing.

It truly is holy ground and sacred space upon which people who are grieving walk. To travel with them is a privilege and a responsibility. To listen well to their stories, to unpack their meaning, and to celebrate the glimmers of hope is something which calls for reverence and sensitivity. Listening for the depth of the pain, for the sparks of light, for puzzlements, for wonderings, and for what is remaining the same are ways of empowering groups to move forward a few steps at a time. The wise planner also knows that regression is part of going in the right direction out of the wilderness zone: three steps forward, two steps back.

For Reflection and Discussion

1. Think of a time when you, as an individual, experienced great loss and went through a period of grieving. What was it like? What was the worst thing about it? What helped you get through it? In the midst of change, what remained the same?

2. Describe an experience when an organization (school, parish, job, association, etc.) to which you belonged went through significant change. What was it like? What effect did it have on the organization? Which of the signs of grieving did you go through as an organization or group? What helped you get through the grieving process?

3. What gifts do you think you have for leading a group through change? How would you use them? To whom would you go in search for gifts you may be lacking, but which are needed by the group?

4. From your experience, what is the power of storytelling and ritual in transitions? How would you incorporate them into the change you may be leading? What value do you see in using storytelling and ritual in transitions?

5. What value do you see in connecting the stories from Scripture with the stories of the people in your group who are going through significant change? When the Scriptures are proclaimed, God speaks. When God speaks, something happens. How would you see using the Scriptures to help people in the grieving process?

CHAPTER

Conversation: the Foundation of Prophetic Planning

Conversation takes time. We need time to sit together, to listen, to worry, and dream together. As this age of turmoil tears us apart, we need to reclaim time to be together. Otherwise, we cannot stop the fragmentation.

MARGARET WHEATLEY

PROPHETIC PLANNING with its fourfold thrust (building on the past, being grounded in faith, conversion and healing, acting boldly) and discerning the will of God for a particular organization can encompass different methods or processes which are all based on quality conversations. The processes encourage as much participation as possible from shareholders—those who participate in and/or benefit from the mission of the organization.

Conversation is at the heart of each of the three planning models described in this chapter. According to Otto Scharmer in *Theory U: Leading from the Future as it Emerges,* there are four different levels of listening: downloading, factual, empathic, and generative. Downloading is probably the most common form of listening. It affirms what one expects to hear. Factual listening is more discriminating. It is open to new information.

Empathic listening stands in the shoes of the other and "feels" with them. Generative listening is the deepest kind of listening. It brings about a change in the listener so that the person is transformed and connected to a deeper source of knowing.

The quality of listening determines the outcomes of groups who plan together. Initially, it is not uncommon to have a great deal of "downloading" listening—people hearing what they want to hear. Gradually, facts begin to be heard and are either denied or affirmed. As relationships are built, empathic listening begins to heal and bond new groups. Generative listening happens when "communion" or grace permeates the environment because individuals truly are reflective and deeply listening within. This kind of listening is powerful in that it allows one to let go of previous convictions and be open to new ways of thinking, relating, and being. As groups are empowered to work together and are guided by deep listening, Prophetic Planning takes root. The following models pull together many aspects of previous chapters into workable ways to do Prophetic Planning.

The three planning models, the "Eight Step Process," the "Retreat Model," and "Appreciative Scenario Building" are some ways to do Prophetic Planning. Each engages people in dialogue based on quality listening. Each invites those most affected by the change to help design what will be new. Each involves understanding the gifts of the past and the current reality, and given that, imagining a preferred future. Each is built on the premise that every organization is a living entity capable of changing and growing.

Each organization is called upon to discern an emerging truth and act in harmony with it through listening, reflecting, and acting. Prophetic Planning is not about rearranging the deck chairs. It is about building capacity for depth and greatness. It is a journey of conversations, both inward and outward. It calls for confidence to look beyond the everyday. It requires humility to recognize the sacred ground of profound change on which organizations may be walking. It is about an exchange of meaning between people who share in the mission of the organization or are influenced by it.

Change recognizes what is trying to emerge, what is trying to grow, what is trying to be released. When observing Michelangelo's unfinished sculptures in Florence, Italy, one vividly sees figures trying to come forward from marble blocks. As one child said to his mother upon seeing the unfinished statue of Saint Matthew, "Mommy, Mommy, look! A man is trying to come out of that rock!" This is what planning is all about—seeing, naming, and acting upon what is emerging for an organization.

The Eight Step Process

The "Eight Step Process" is one that can be used organically with large organizations that are facing emerging challenges. It is designed for organizations that value input based on conversations with shareholders from the grass roots. The process is based on the belief that people can and are willing to help create their own futures. The eight steps are constructed on the principles of learning communities, where people come together for conversation with questions and data and acquire new knowledge and insights. Through the conversation process, they discover trends, deepen their understanding of their organization, and learn what it is to become and then build the future.

The Eight Step Process outlined below is a proven successful method for helping Catholic dioceses move forward in strengthening parish life, given the need for good stewardship of resources. It is also successfully applied to nonprofits or communities of vowed religious.

The process lends itself to the renewal of the whole organization. At the parish level, it is an invitation to be in conversation about the basic questions of who we are and why we exist. How do we mirror the presence of God and respond to God's gifts? How do we best use our human and financial resources? From a diocesan perspective, it provides opportunities for the diocese to be more effective in carrying out its mission and using its resources.

For the process to work properly, there needs to be an appointed planning commission of respected leaders who are charged with the oversight of the whole project. In Catholic dioceses, the bishop appoints the commission, meets with the priests to ensure they are oriented to the process, articulates the goals of the process, and monitors progress. The bishop also approves the criteria upon which suggestions are made and the models of parish configurations that are appropriate for the future vitality of the diocese.

Ultimately, the planning commission, after studying data and attentively listening to the clusters of parishes, makes recommendations to the bishop related to the emerging picture of how parishes might be reorganized in the future. Models such as partnership, linkage, consolidations, and using parish directors or teams often emerge as viable for the future. Through the process, parishes are given parameters upon which to look at their realities. They are given criteria upon which to assess themselves, as well as prayer and faith-sharing resources. The assumptions the commission is working from are made public. The process is transparent and rooted in faith, conversion, and healing.

Pastors are asked to appoint a core team of four people (pastor plus four) to help guide the planning process through the following steps. After individual parishes work alone and evaluate what they are currently doing, they begin to work with their neighbors in clusters.

Conversation

At the parish and cluster level, these conversations lead to an evaluation of the current reality, an assessment of the quality of parish/cluster ministry, and an initial look toward the future.

Cluster Suggestion

The cluster suggestion is based on one of the models for the future approved by the bishop and made with a rationale by the cluster to the planning commission.

Preliminary Recommendation

The planning commission reviews all cluster suggestions, develops preliminary recommendations in light of identified criteria, and sends them back to each cluster of parishes for a response.

Conversation

This conversation focuses on the preliminary recommendation at the cluster level and the preparation of a response.

Response

The response to the preliminary recommendation with a rationale by the cluster is made to the planning commission.

Final Recommendation

Following review of the response, the final recommendation is made to the bishop by the planning commission.

Decision

After further consultation, the bishop makes a decision on the final recommendations made to him by the planning commission.

Implementation

This step involves a series of actions to carry out the decisions made by the bishop, which are based on the recommendations and suggestions from the clusters and the planning commission. It incorporates articulating the mission, values, vision, goals, and objectives, as well as action steps and timelines, which need to live in the future.

Throughout the process, the parishes and clusters of parishes take on the role of learning communities in conversation with each other. They pray, share faith, listen attentively, and are engaged in answering powerful questions about who they are and who they are called to be.

As learning communities, there will be many ways for parishioners to be involved, such as town hall meetings, parish assemblies, committee work, focus groups, etc. Materials and processes are incorporated by core and cluster committees to empower parish leaders to implement strategies for getting people involved.

The Eight Step Process brings about significant organizational change by promoting dialogue and conversations among all shareholders, which deepens the community's understanding of itself, its faith, and its future. Learning communities nurture gracious space, promote a curiosity, and tap into hidden energy. They court compassion and empathy and do everything possible to ensure that there are "no winners and losers," only people willing to take risks to create a better future for all. The process builds on conversations of shared meaning and motivates participants to work for the common good, to be shareholders in the reign of God.

Some of the strengths of the Eight Step Process include:

■ The process builds ownership of those affected by the change.

■ The wisdom of the community/organization is incorporated in the decisions for the future, thus enhancing the quality of the decisions.

■ The process helps the community/organization deepen its understanding of who it is and who it is called to become.

■ The process makes the community more conscious of the realities it and its leaders face.

■ The process shares the burden of decision making between leaders and the community or organization, thus lessening the pressure on the leaders.

■ The process respectfully combines the past, the present, and the future.

■ The process involves the community in discerning the will of God for the future.

The Retreat Model for Nonprofits, Parishes and Schools

The "Retreat Model" anchors transformational change in the ability of people to come together to pray and to share faith, stories, and symbols, as well as listen with openness and understanding. A broad spectrum of the community is invited to articulate the emerging mission, values, vision, goals, and objectives of an organization. The model provides opportunities for conversations and attentive listening about the real issues facing the organization, hospital, parish, school, or diocese. It allows for the development of strategies to transform challenges into opportunities. Direction is set by developing the mission, values, and vision of the organization. This is followed by looking at issues facing the group, setting goals, and examining programs. For the goals to become operational, they need objectives. Developing the mission, values, and vision statements, as well as goals and objectives, is the work of the retreats. Creating the action steps and overseeing the accountability for the plan is the work of the administration and/or board of the organization.

The Retreat Model calls for a "futuring team" to oversee the process and make decisions, not only about the process, but also about the plan to be forwarded to the governing person or body for a decision. That committee meets regularly to advise whoever is facilitating the planning process and to provide direction. The Retreat Model usually entails two to three one-and-a-half day gathering experiences. This may include "overnights" or not. The model calls for gathering leaders and consumers of the services of the organization. In a parish or school situation, that includes staff, parish council, pastor, committee members, community leaders, and interested parishioners who may have held leadership positions in the past. In nonprofit associations, organizational leaders, staff, volunteers, board members, community leaders, governmental representatives, and recipients of the services provided by the organization are included. The Retreat Model also can be used for clusters of parishes or organizations which have similar missions, as well as the single entities noted above.

This model lends itself to participation of all members of an organization by using focus groups and/or electronic survey instruments over the Internet. Issues can be surfaced, various draft statements of planning documents can be critiqued, and suggestions can be made by all constituents for the futuring team to consider. It promotes broad participation and ultimately ownership of the plan.

In preparation for the first retreat, a pre-retreat survey is sent out to all interested parties in which they are asked to give input into evaluative aspects of the organization and offer ideas for mission, values, vision, goals, and objectives. This valuable input is used to begin the planning process. The retreats are dynamic processes which further conversation, prompt new insights, and help bond the community.

After the initial retreat, a first draft of the plan is generated from the input, sharings, conversations, and deliberations that happened at the retreat. This is distributed to the community electronically and/or in hard copy for feedback. Various committees, boards, and councils look at it, converse about it, and perhaps struggle with it and give their critique, suggestions, and general reactions.

From these conversations, a new draft is created and further conversations are held about the plan at a second retreat. These conversations challenge people to extend themselves to open their minds and hearts to new ideas and to let go of some of the "way we have always done things" approaches.

The conversations point to the messiness of planning. The wilderness zone has paths which dead end. Huge rocks obstruct our vision. Things are not neat and tidy. There are disruptions in the wilderness. There will not always be clear categories. The value of meaningful conversations based on deep listening in the wilderness is that they breed strong relationships, new ideas, courageous stances, etc.

Retreats give us time to notice what is going on. They help us restore hope and give us opportunities to think about and share what is going on in the world, both in our own and in the larger world. They provide an environment where we can articulate our needs, the needs of our families, and the families of the world. Margaret Wheatley notes that we do not have to have the same answers, but if we are asking the same questions, we can begin to change things, to transform organizations, and ultimately the world. This is what planning is all about.

The second retreat builds on conversations begun at the first one. The integration of prayer, storytelling, and symbol sharing points to the extraordinary in the ordinary, the sacred in the secular, and to seeing the "more" in life. These kinds of activities enrich conversations about the meaning and purpose of organizations, whether they are spiritual, civic, or secular. They are the glue holding together the organizations. They support the more measurable aspects of planning. Activities incorporated into planning retreats often include "fish bowls" and "wisdom walls," where issues can be discussed in some depth and ideas shared that relate to each other. Some groups have a third retreat, where more time for conversation can be spent on building action steps for the future.

Some of the strengths of the Retreat Model include the following:

■ There is inclusion of both "left and right" brain activities.

■ The process takes into account the whole person and incorporates reflection, ritual, and storytelling.

■ Various learning styles are incorporated into the process to meet the needs of visual learners, auditory learners, kinesthetic learners, and those who learn best by interacting with others.

■ Multiple viewpoints are encouraged. The environment is set so people speak respectfully but honestly about their concerns and issues. Attentive listening at all levels enhances the quality of the planning.

■ Mistakes and failures of the past are seen as opportunities to learn for the future.

■ There is a willingness to break old ways of doing things and experiment with new ones.

■ People have a broad view of the organization beyond their special interest or involvement.

▪ People leave the retreat experience more engaged in the parish, cluster, or organization.

▪ New relationships have formed, which continue to energize the organization.

▪ Direction is set for the organization with user-friendly goals and objectives, as well as measureable action plans.

Appreciative Scenario Building

"Appreciative Inquiry" was developed more than twenty years ago by David Cooperrider at Case Western Reserve University School of Business. It is a conversational process of asking questions in a way that brings forth the good that already exists in an organization, group, or individual. Its thrust is to enhance the positive things which are already happening and to deepen an understanding of them. Appreciative Inquiry is the antithesis of a problem-solving method of planning.

Appreciative Inquiry is built on a very positive approach linking to past successes. It is highly participative, engages in storytelling, and uses interviewing as one of its preferred techniques. It is imaginative and stimulates vision and creativity. It is sometimes described as the 4-D approach to planning: Discovery, Dreaming, Designing and Destiny. Appreciative Inquiry is based on the use of powerful questions to stimulate new thinking, as well as the bonding of different groups within the organization.

Discovery focuses on appreciating what is. What is the best thing happening in our parish, our community, our organization? What attracted you to our community? Tell a story about a time when you were proud to be a member of our team, parish, community, or organization. What were your hopes and dreams when you decided to join us? What keeps you here? When do you feel most passionate about being with us or working with us?

Dreaming imagines what could be. It builds on discovery by augmenting the possibilities of what has been generated there. It calls for people to envision a better world. It seeks to expand the organization's potential. It might ask: "What would happen if...?" The dream phase challenges the status quo. Through sharing the dreams in conversation with others, synergy and excitement are released. The thrust of this phase is to facilitate a dialogue among shareholders that creates energy for the future. This is followed by starting to discern common themes or life-giving forces among all the participants' dreams.

The third phase is the Design phase. There are four steps here: select design elements, identify internal and external relationships, identify themes and engage in conversation, and write provocative propositions. This phase names internal and external associations (employees, clients, etc.) themes such as customer satisfaction and employee expectations, space needs, training, ministry realities, and issues related to the dreams. This leads to provocative propositions related to the relationships and themes noted above.

The final phase is Destiny. It deals with "what will be." The focus is often on how to empower, learn, adjust, and improvise. Depending upon what themes have emerged, results of this phase are action plans that may call for such things as a mentorship program, career planning, new programs, new orientation of employees, an "in-house university," partnering for ministries, etc.

Appreciative Inquiry's strengths are found particularly in its first two phases: Discovery and Dreaming. There the stories of the community are shared; what is working well is highlighted and proclaimed; new connections are made between the organization's divisions; hopes and concerns are articulated; dreams are formed and shared; the community is energized for the future.

While the Design and Destiny phases of Appreciative Inquiry may serve many organizations well, scenario building coalesces some of the dynamics from the Discovery and Dreaming phases and focuses the group's energy to zero in on creating a future within a limited amount of time. Scenario Building's strengths are found in its ability to anticipate different future developments. It can take the "dreams" of Appreciative Inquiry and ask, "What happens if...?" It simplifies the Design and Destiny phases and incorporates some analytical thinking into the process.

By taking the best elements of Appreciative Inquiry and Scenario Building, which was discussed in Chapter Six, an effective hybrid can serve the community well. The Appreciative Scenario Building approach includes:

1. Enhancing awareness and deepening the organization or the community's appreciation for what has been and what is. This includes storytelling, recalling the past, and sharing deeply held values.

2. Imagining what could be in the future. Focusing on the key components of the future, which give life to the group, helps shape the future.

3. Forming different scenarios based on various external and internal factors begins to present options for the future. Asking significant questions and testing the assumptions upon which each scenario is based is critical at this juncture.

4. Choosing which scenario will best serve the organization. This is done based on pre-determined criteria such as financial viability, the availability of human resources, etc.

5. Implementing the scenario. Develop action steps to execute the scenario.

This model has been successfully used with groups around the country who only have access to each other via conference calls and the Internet. Sharing summaries of interviews where great stories were heard, communicating about scenarios proposed for the future, critiquing scenarios, prioritizing them, etc. can all be done electronically using appropriate survey instruments. The point is not to eliminate face-to-face conversations. Sometimes the electronic survey work is done in preparation for these meetings. At other times it is done as an inclusive gesture to get as much wisdom and input as possible when otherwise geographical location would prevent participation.

Some of the strengths of the Appreciative Scenario Building include the following.

■ Builds upon the successes of the past.

■ Energizes groups to set direction by telling successful stories, building upon meaningful conversations, and gaining deeper understanding of those things which give life to the organization or community.

■ Encourages conversation about the various options available for the future.

■ Combines intuitive, imaginative, and analytical approaches.

■ Focuses on a realistic and bold future.

■ Engages people to envision the future in several ways. Through conversation, it helps groups consider the impact various scenarios will have on them. It helps people anticipate developments and changes they may not otherwise have noticed.

■ Helps the group consider which strategies will be most effective, courageous, and prudent, given different future directions.

No matter which process is used, or if others are used which have not been described here, an essential element in Prophetic Planning is meaningful conversations with those who will be affected by the anticipated change. Powerful questions, criteria, and broad parameters all help focus significant dialogue among those involved in the planning process. Sharing faith, stories, symbols, and meaningful dialogue are at the heart of successful planning because they holistically integrate the spiritual, emotional, physical, human, and analytical dimensions of planning. The spiritual dimensions of faith-based groups that are found in the Bible and Koran, as well as other sacred writings and symbols, contribute to the strength and life of the planning groups. The value-laden foundations of non-faith based groups are located in their founding documents, original principles, mission, values, and vision. These often become a source of inspiration for those leading non-faith-based organizations.

For Reflection and Discussion

1. What do you see as the value in empowering those affected by change to be part of the change process? What elements do you think need to be in place for a participative process to work well?

2. Think of a planning situation in which you have been involved. If your success was completely guaranteed, what bold steps might you consider doing?

3. What conversations, if begun today, could open up new possibilities for the future?

4. How might you use or adapt any of the processes identified in this chapter in your planning challenges?

5. What assumptions do you need to test or challenge when beginning a planning process? What is the value in testing assumptions?

CHAPTER **8**

Creating a Culture of Prophetic Planning and Effective Action

If I knew planning could be this productive and this much fun, I would be much more committed to planning efforts.

A RECENT CLIENT

Culture of Planning

THE PROPHETIC PLANNING JOURNEY is not always productive or fun. In fact, sometimes the best laid plans wind up on dusty shelves or lost somewhere in an office drawer. Creation of healthy attitudes toward the planning process itself is one important factor that makes a big difference in efforts that bear good fruit or initiatives that cost valuable time and money, but go nowhere.

In this chapter, we will explore the notion that one important task for leaders is to develop and nurture a positive and valued culture of planning, as well as effective implementation of the plans throughout their organizations. Some organizations have already developed a culture of planning throughout the various levels within the college or parish or nonprofit. Too many other organizations, however, do not have a positive and successful history with past planning initiatives or simply refuse to engage in any formal planning initiatives at all.

Some leaders seem more focused on maintaining the status quo or just surviving challenging times, while others are deeply committed to transforming their current reality into something new and creative for the common good in their own communities and beyond and to thriving in the midst of all the challenges and changes around them. Why is this so? Many times, leaders are unfamiliar with the key elements necessary for a healthy culture of planning to exist. Some of these elements include:

■ Encouraging participation by shareholders throughout the organization and listening to their hopes and concerns in a genuine manner.

■ Acting consistently as a learning organization willing to gain insight from past successes and struggles, while applying these insights to present realities and challenges.

■ Promoting effective communication characterized by both honesty and respect.

■ Having the courage to explore the tough questions and address any "elephants in the room," so that all the critical issues are discussed.

■ Creating multiple opportunities for forums or other approaches to bringing people together to explore the hopes, concerns, realities, and challenges facing the organization.

We will now explore the meaning of diversity, culture, and co-culture and what is required for organizations to embrace a culture of planning. We will then apply these understandings to the realities of planning, change, and conflict.

The Meaning of Culture

One way to approach an understanding of culture is through definitions of three distinct and related terms: diversity, culture, and co-culture.

Diversity is a word that means "all the ways we are different as human beings" and can be divided into external and internal differences. In general, external differences are the easiest to notice, while internal differences are the most significant. These differences can be summarized as follows:

- External differences: physical attributes, visible physical disabilities, dress, musical interests, speech patterns, mannerisms, etc.

- Internal differences: values, customs, history, personality, beliefs, place of origin, learning styles, world view, sexual orientation, various types of ability and disability, hobbies, habits, etc.

Eric Law, an Episcopalian priest and author of several books on diversity and culture, uses the image of an iceberg to illustrate the impact of external and internal differences. While the external differences or "above the surface" tip of the iceberg are forces to be reckoned with, it is what lies "below the surface" that has the greatest impact. When trust and respect for our differences exist to a high degree in an organization, they are experienced as sources of richness. Conversely, when trust and respect do not exist at all or only to a minimal degree, diversity or differences are experienced as threats to the status quo.

There are many definitions for the meaning of the word "culture." One favorite is from A.J. Marsella: "Culture is a learned behavior which is transmitted from one generation to another for purposes of promoting individual and social survival, adaptation, growth, and development." A shorthand way of thinking about culture is to think of it as "the way we do things around here."

One organization may be very casual in how folks dress at work. For example, at Microsoft, blue jeans are often the norm, while coats and ties for men and dresses for women are rare. IBM or the FBI, on the hand, are well known as workplaces where white shirts, coats, and ties are the standard attire for men, while women are expected to "dress up." In similar fashion, some organizations maintain formal records of transactions from years and even decades past, while other organizations barely keep up with their recordkeeping responsibilities. While differences themselves are not good or bad, they are all significant and have much to teach us.

While genuine differences in organizations are definitely manifested in styles of dress or in a variety of work styles, they are profoundly represented in various approaches to planning. If represented on a continuum, they might range from "make it up and make it happen" planning on one end of the continuum to "periodic or every few years" planning in the middle of the continuum to "ongoing or a very consistent culture" of planning as learning on the other end of the continuum.

Some important questions are: How often is a culture of planning embraced by leaders and organizations, and what allows this culture of planning to thrive? Sadly, in our experience working with many leaders and organizations, far too many people have only a limited understanding of the word "culture" and do not view it as connected at all to planning. Rather, they understand culture as simply referring to one's ethnic or racial heritage. While ethnicity is an important meaning of culture to be sure, it is in truth just one dimension of many.

This is why we have found much of value in learning from the work of L. Samovar and R. Porter. They have taken culture ("the way we do things around here") and added to its meaning with a new term: co-culture. A co-culture involves groups or social communities exhibiting communication characteristics, perceptions, values, beliefs, and practices that are significantly different enough to distinguish them from the other groups, communities, and the dominant culture. Members of co-cultures also share some patterns and perceptions with the larger population.

This means that individuals have many co-cultures including ethnicity, age, birth order, vocation, hobbies, marital status, sexual orientation, and more. In the same way, organizations can be said to have many co-cultures as well, including leadership styles, age groups, professions, work styles, and more. When the meaning of co-cultures is applied to organizations, it broadens the approach in Prophetic Planning to include many different dimensions of organizational life.

To embrace an effective culture of planning, leaders and organizations must come to an understanding and commitment that planning is an ongoing reality. A strong organization will facilitate increasing levels of new learning through detailed strategies for both planning and implementation. In addition, through the regular monitoring of expected performance and of frequent evaluation of actual performance, new insights will emerge that then are funneled back into the next planning cycle.

One practical way to engage the concept of dealing with differences and co-cultures is through the use of co-cultural mapping. Dr. Cleo Molina, a consultant with The Reid Group, has developed an exercise for co-cultural mapping that is useful to groups and organizations.

Personal Co-Cultural Mapping

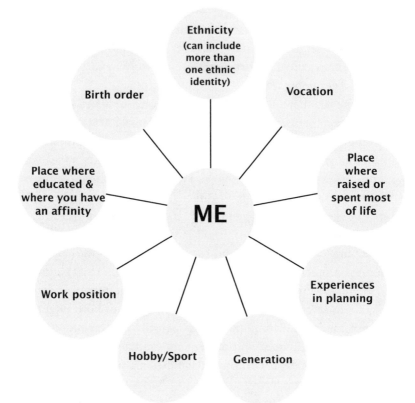

The graphic illustrates the complexity of what contributes to each person's co-culture. Ethnic heritage, with its traditions and rituals, helps shape each one of us and contributes greatly to our identity. Our vocation or calling beckons us to develop a skill set to be successful in what we feel we are called to do. The place where we were raised helps shape our outlook on the world. Being raised in the southern part of the United States presents a different set of experiences than being raised in the north with its snowy and harsh winters. Experiences in planning affects the attitudes one brings to faith-based or nonprofit planning experiences. Some people are natural planners in all aspects of their lives. Others rarely plan. For instance, some save for retirement, while others rarely think of life beyond work. Each generation has its own set of values and perspectives, by which its members view the world. Those who lived during the violent protests of the 60s have very different perspectives than those who are the young adults of today.

Hobbies and sports help mold our skills and affect our ideas about success and failure. Work positions create within one certain expectations. If I'm in a leadership role, I may expect to be recognized as a leader at home and in volunteer service. If I'm in a supporting role at work, I may expect to be in the same role at home or in my work in a ministry. Education plays an important role in our learned behavior. The experience of going to a particular high school or college forms people socially, spiritually, and academically. Those shared values are often very influential beyond the educational events. Much has been written about the influence of birth order. There are certain characteristics of the oldest, the youngest, and middle children that seem to be based only on the order in which one was born in a family. This is also true of the only child.

By knowing one's co-culture and learning the co-culture of others, people can begin to see what they have in common and where many differences are. This understanding helps create communities of mutual trust amidst many differences. It helps bond communities. It energizes people for Prophetic Planning.

Organizational Co-Cultural Mapping

Individuals in planning groups can not only make and share their own co-cultural map, but each of them also can make and share an organizational co-culture map from their perspective, which can be a very profound experience. Each of the aspects can be important to any given group. For instance, if a group has had to relocate to a new worship site, school, office, or health care location, that has or will influence the culture of the group. If people have had negative experiences of planning that will be reflected in their attitude to the planning process at hand, or if some in the group are used to certain rituals such as beginning meetings with "rounds" or "prayer" that is not the norm of the current group, these things may cause distress. Leadership styles can help meld a group or make it dysfunctional, depending on expectations and experience brought to the group. Creative co-cultural analysis is helpful because it brings together new and useful information about both individuals and organizations. When this new information is combined with significant trust and respect among leaders throughout an organization, the foundation has been set for a meaningful culture of planning to flourish. This is not enough, however. In addition to establishing a culture of planning, there must be a strong commitment to effective communication. Solid principles of communication are discussed in Chapter Three.

One of the great advantages of doing co-cultural mapping is that it provides an opportunity for people to know each other at a deeper level than is often experienced in non-permanent work groups. The tool lends itself to understanding differences and can be the basis for forming a learning community.

Characteristics of Learning Communities

Learning communities are formed when organizations operate out of a culture of shared visions and talents. They become highly productive because they share talents and vision and develop a group synergy that is based on shared intelligence, convictions, and values. Learning communities form a secure home for a culture of planning.

Live by a Shared Vision

What is it that we want to look like in five years? If we hold a common vision—one that is energizing and satisfying—it will be easy for a group to coalesce around that forward movement. If an organization has not envisioned its future, that is the first step to creating a learning community. If it lives out its mission and values, what will it be in the future?

Engage in Positive Imaging

Seeing things in a positive light energizes learning communities. Reframing the way we look at things in a new light so the affirming aspects can influence our thinking is a distinguishing mark of a learning community. This is not "pie in the sky" thinking. Rather it is a focus on what is positive in any situation. Sometimes it means looking at the situation from the one thousand feet perspective, rather than the fifty feet perspective. Sometimes it means imagining what the situation could become in three to five years. An organization cannot even think about planning for the future until it can imagine, even in the wilderness zone, a constructive positive change.

Encourage Creative Thinking

Learning communities promote creative thinking. Does the group's climate invite all to look at ways to do things better? How is creative thinking acknowledged and rewarded? To create a true learning community where Prophetic Planning can flourish, one needs to create an environment where it is safe to "think out loud." Three things encourage creative thinking: 1) a structure for positive interactions; 2) an environment where members can solve their own problems; 3) a public acknowledgement of successful creative solutions to problems.

Support Boldness

"Safe" parishes, schools, colleges, and other organizations where risk-taking is not valued are doomed to stagnate and diminish. Learning organizations that embrace Prophetic Planning are ones where risk-taking is not only tolerated, it is encouraged. How can we be ten times bolder? This kind of thinking in learning communities unleashes potential. Sometimes individuals or small groups initiate the first bold thinking. To nurture and refine the boldness, they need a supportive community of co-learners with whom they can explore the boldness. Risk-taking is rooted in intuition and imagery. What would it look like if we were…? Learning communities support boldness, because no one person is the risk-taker—the community is. The community shines when successes occur and is supportive when boldness does not reach the desired results.

Six Insights That Contribute to a Culture of Planning

Believing in the significance of planning as learning and committing to an ongoing process of planning and learning is a critical first step.

1. Recognizing the need for good communication and opportunities for sharing on a significant level help form communities supportive of the culture of planning.

2. There is power in differences. Dealing with differences by showing respect and encouraging various perspectives can lead to dynamic and creative ways of working together for the good of the organization.

3. Using co-cultural mapping particularly focused on the organization can begin to build bonds of understanding, acceptance of differences, and increasing levels of trust and respect.

4. Forming learning communities helps guarantee a continual culture of planning.

5. Building on the strengths of the past gives energy for the future, while considering opportunities to promote healing and reconciliation is a genuine gift available throughout a planning process.

6. Reflecting on all that the people in the organization share in common gives a healthy foundation to addressing the important things that may be experienced as challenging differences.

As important as planning is to an organization in moving through the wilderness zone and into a real and meaningful new beginning, it remains at its best a crucial means to accomplishing a larger end.

The end is most often experienced as a creative and dynamic implementation process. The true goal of any effective planning process is not a "perfect" action plan, but rather an action plan that empowers leaders and their organizations to be more faithful and effective in living out their mission and values. This happens in Prophetic Planning processes, while there is also a commitment to achieve multiple goals and live into one's vision that is prophetic, "ten times bolder," and inspiring.

For Reflection and Discussion

1. In your mind, what are the basic ingredients for creating a culture of planning? Which of these elements are already in your organization?

2. In what way do differences enhance your organization? What are some key ways to deal with differences so that they are perceived to be positive forces and not negative ones?

3. How do you think understanding co-cultures contributes to effective planning groups?

4. How would you describe your organization's co-culture, using the diagram as a starter?

5. How is your planning group a learning community? In what ways could it enhance the culture of planning?

CHAPTER **9**

Pulling It All Together— a Spiritual Journey

May the God of hope fill you with all joy and peace in believing, so that you may abound in hope by the power of the Holy Spirit.

ROMANS 15:13

WE HAVE TAKEN A JOURNEY, an exploration through Prophetic Planning, and seen its intersection with change and transformation as well as with conflict and resistance to change. Planning is a journey toward the common good. It is the learning community that takes the journey, filled with the hope of making a significant, positive difference in the world. The community becomes aware of what its values are, what its purpose is, what its vision for the future is, and how it is going to achieve its purpose and its vision. The community "thinks together" with both its head and its heart in order to create new habits of action.

We have walked through what at times seemed like barren land—where only conflict lives and the potential for "winners" and "losers" abounds. At other times, we have been led by a pillar of fire and the cloudy times seem like many "yesterdays" ago. We have circumvented huge rocks, which seemed to block our straight paths, and we have squeaked through narrow gates. We have felt at times like immigrants and refugees in foreign lands. We have been fearful and mournful as we let go of people and things we had grown to love. At times we felt like both pioneers and settlers simultaneously taking up residence in strange lands. At other times we have experienced peace and joy and the power of the Spirit.

Lessons From the Prophetic Planning Journey

Openness to Mystery

We have learned to be open to the mystery of Prophetic Planning, to the surprises along the way, to the Spirit's presence. The creativity that has emerged from respectful dialogue has engendered new ways to see things. The barren desert has begun to bloom. Hope has been engaged. Stability has been restored.

Prophetic Planning has led us to remember and value the past. In our imaginations, we have walked with those who have founded our organizations, institutions, parishes, schools, and health care facilities. We have come to know the sacrifices they made in the early years. That helped us connect our sacrifices with theirs. That connectedness gave us a sense of solidarity with those who have gone before us. That bondedness has opened doors to the mystery of the dilemmas we face today.

We have seen that Prophetic Planning is based on faith. It is a process whereby we encounter God, much like Elijah did, by climbing the mountain, and through prayer, listening for the whispers of the Spirit. And like Elijah, we are called back to the community to listen to the Spirit speaking in and through those gathered to assist with planning.

In non-faith-based groups, we believe that there is "more to life than meets the eye," which underlies successful planning efforts. The energy that comes from living out an organization's deeply-held values and beliefs—the energy of transformation, no matter what its acknowledged source—is present both in the letting go and building upon the past, the molding of the future, and the mystery of the present. We have become aware of our own conversions, our releasing of cherished moments and events, and our own change process. We also have grown to recognize our need for healing and the community's need for healing, which are all part of the process of Prophetic Planning. In all Prophetic Planning processes, there is a need to deal with the mystery of loss and pain and the promise of new life.

In parish and school settings, often it is the loss of symbols which for years have pointed to and embodied the "something more" in life for which we grieve. It can be a comfort-giving worship space where all the stained glass windows have "spoken" to us for years. We recall how they look when the sun hits them in the summer and how they look in the darkness of winter. There God was present to us in a special way. And while intellectually we know God is not contained in a certain space, emotionally that special space is where we have become aware of God's presence in a profound way.

We have "tried on" being bolder—ten times bolder. We imagined how things could be different if we were ten times bolder. We have tested the waters in regard to boldness. When is it foolhardy? When is it prophetic? When does it respond to the Spirit's call? When is it merely a focus on self-aggrandizement? We have come to realize that timidity is not part of Prophetic Planning. As T.S. Eliot reminds us, "Only those who will risk going too far can possibly find out how far one can go."

We have experienced in faith-based planning groups the agonizing process of trying to discern the will of God. We have been attentive to the moaning and groaning of the Spirit trying to penetrate the psyches of those who led planning efforts. We have seen "dimly" (I Corinthians 13:12), as in a fog, as we began to decipher where the Spirit is in the messiness of Prophetic Planning. We have spent the forty days in the desert in our journey from darkness to light. We have "run the race" and experienced faith as "the realization of what is hoped for and evidence of things not seen" (Hebrews 11:1).

All Prophetic Planning groups go through a discernment process, always asking what is best for the organization. In some cases, the organizations need to amend their structures, mission, and vision in order to live out their values in changing times. In other times, they need to expand and embrace new realities. Still at other times, they are called to celebrate what they have been able to accomplish and end their existence with dignity and gratitude. Openness to the mysteries encountered in the planning process ensures comprehensive and solid plans for the future.

Prophetic Planning as a Continual Process

While there are definite periods in individual lives and organizational existence where the focus is on various aspects of planning and implementation of plans, we know that the cycle of planning, evaluating, and expediting strategies is ongoing.

Planning is a constant process because change and transformation are a lasting part of all life. Change has considerable impact on people. It can bring fear and anxiety, hope and inspiration. Change is an inevitable part of life. How we interpret and deal with change is what brings meaning and purpose in life. The change cycle involves new beginnings. These are often rooted in the past, nurtured in the present, and bring us to the future. Planning makes the future happen so that it can be understood and meaningfully integrated into the purpose of life. Transformation begins when we realize that something is changing. Like Dorothy in the Wizard of Oz, we realize we aren't in Kansas—or anywhere else familiar—anymore.

Change is the jolt that unsettles the *status quo*. It forces individuals and communities to discover what is really important. On the journey, we experienced change as beckoning us forward to articulate what we really care about. We let ourselves experience the clouds of uncertainties with the hope that in that mass a star would be born and new life would emerge. It was in the wilderness zone that we brooded about our future, hoping against hope that things could stay the same. It was in the chaos of the wilderness that we began to imagine how things might be changed, and eventually also how the future could be life-giving and nurturing.

The journey from endings to new beginnings was a circuitous route. Often we could not "make straight the way" as we could not see the end point. Our memories helped us to make the past present in such a way that it nourished us and helped us have hope for a future that would also be purposeful. When we were distracted in the wilderness, we found that opportunities presented themselves to get to know other pilgrims, listen to their stories, be attentive to their hopes and fears, and ultimately discover our common goals, hopes, and dreams. It was this awareness that bonded us to each other and helped us initiate building a future together. By walking with each other and sharing what really matters, we crossed barriers together. We were able to let go of self-pity, engage in meaningful dialogue, and transform losses into opportunities that were never possible before we entered the wilderness.

The losses were ritualized. Stories were told related to them. They became the seeds of the future that would be watered and nurtured by the new community planting them.

Stresses Along the Way

All journeys have their stressors. When young children are but a few miles on the trip, they begin to ask: "Are we there yet?" Some will always want to move quickly through planning. They may be more ready for the end result. They may think they know the exact route. They may be impatient by nature.

Time can be big stressor. Meeting aggressive timelines often causes stress in groups. Scheduling can be a nightmare, if too many people are on a planning committee or subcommittee. On the other hand, stretching out a planning process too long can lead to decreased momentum and eventual apathy. Often when people take long trips, they will comment at the end, "It was about a week too long"—meaning the energy and pleasure of the trip had diminished and it seemed more like going through the motions by the time it was over.

Most successful planning efforts for an individual organization, parish, or school can be successfully accomplished within three to nine months, if the process is comprehensive and laid out well. When working with large and complex organizations such as dioceses and school systems, it usually takes nine to twelve months of planning, plus another six months of developing the implementation plans. Timelines for planning need to be tailored to the individual situation. Having timelines is good. Building in flexibility is essential. Holding one another accountable for meeting the timelines is at the heart of successful Prophetic Planning.

Conflict can be another stressor on the planning journey. Every family vacation has its conflicts. They can revolve around minor issues such as "Where will we eat lunch?" to more important issues like those involving safety or health. As noted in a previous chapter, conflict is a natural part of life. How we deal with it is most important. Respectfully disagreeing and striving to come to mutual understanding, embracing a position that is a "win-win," is the most desirable result of disagreements or conflicts.

Often conflict arises when there is resistance to change that has gone unnoticed or has not been addressed well. Resisting change is not bad in itself. Sometimes it is good to resist change. Such resistance fosters new thinking and different decisions where the options earlier rejected become acceptable. As someone once noted, a kite flies against the wind, not with it. Great ideas have come from initial resistance to change. Resistance paralyzes individuals or groups when all the energy is focused on maintaining the *status quo,* and there is not sufficient openness to new ideas or approaches or meaningful dialogue.

A third stressor in Prophetic Planning is lack of effective leadership. When people attempt to lead a major planning process who are unorganized or do not have well-honed communication skills, groups often become lethargic, conflictual, disheartened, or self-destructive. One way to enhance planning efforts is to invite co-leaders or co-facilitators and provide ongoing coaching. This not only enhances the group's accomplishments, but it also relieves the pressure on the planning leaders.

On the journey, we noted that the skills, knowledge, and abilities most needed by planning leaders included:

▪ The ability to include all segments of people who will be affected by the planning results in the process.

▪ Knowledge and skills in laying out the planning process so that it is clear what steps need to be taken and who needs to be involved in each step along the way.

▪ Excellent communication skills, especially listening—not only to the head, but to the heart.

▪ Ability to think systemically—to see how parts and the whole interrelate.

▪ Good organizational abilities so the tasks are clear.

▪ Ability to delegate and call people to accountability.

▪ Ability to inspire others.

▪ Ability to facilitate conflict management.

▪ An imagination that pictures a meaningful and purposeful future life for the organization.

▪ Ability to see "more than meets the eye."

▪ The ability to be a positive force in the process affirming all the good work of others.

Lack of flexibility is the fourth planning stressor. Plans need to fit groups. Adjustments in all proven planning processes are often required. There is no one way that a "best practice" for planning does not need to be adapted to individual groups. Forcing groups into rigid planning processes leads to failure. One size never fits all. On the planning journey, "Implement and improve" is a good mantra. Flexibility does not mean being "whishy-washy" and indecisive. It means that schedules, leadership styles, and steps in the process can be adjusted based on the needs of a particular group. Flexibility points to the focus being on people and their needs, not the process, as a determining factor.

Flexibility includes acknowledging the uncomfortable nature of change and transitions. It includes staying the course, knowing when to take a break, having a sense of humor, and basic self-confidence to believe in a positive end point.

Connecting Along the Way

Prophetic Planning presents many opportunities to deepen relationships with others on the journey. New relationships are forged as people who were once strangers get to know one another and discover all they have in common. Attention to others' values, dreams, fears, and histories brings new awareness of the commonality of human life.

In faith-based groups, especially in the Judeo-Christian tradition, prayer is what holds the group together. It is not a matter of "saying prayers." Prayer is a process of sharing with one another and connecting with God in an explicit way. In Christian planning groups, proclaiming the Scriptures of the day or the Sunday, reflecting on how God is speaking to those gathered, and sharing the words which had particular meaning to each person is a way of not only connecting to God, but bonding with one another. When the Scriptures are proclaimed, God is speaking. When God speaks, something happens. It is the God of yesteryear who led the people through the wilderness to the Promised Land. It is the God of today who leads those gathered in the name of a gracious God through the wilderness of loss, letting go, hurt, and conversion. It is the God of tomorrow who has promised to always be with us through the presence of the Spirit.

Prayer that includes the Scriptures and faith sharing has powerful consequences in the planning process. First of all, it is dialogue with God. God speaks through the Word. We reflect on the meaning of the Word for us today. We share that with each other. In that sharing, a window is opened to the soul, a window which helps others know who we are and who we strive to become. It is a communal form of prayer where the community is enriched and guided through the proclamation of the Word of God. The community is bonded to God and one another through the Spirit's presence. The group often concludes its prayer with general intercessions where it remembers those who have gone before, those in need, the larger church, and the world. The group goes beyond its personal needs and requests God to care for all peoples. Often the group finishes its prayer with the prayer Jesus taught.

All faith-based groups have rituals, writings, and inspirational pieces which they have inherited from their founders or those who have gone before them. These can all be used to inspire the planning group and give it direction, as well as bond the group members who may not know each other into a productive working group. Including prayers for wisdom for the planning process at regular worship not only alerts the community to the need for prayerful support, but it also reminds people of the potential for change which may result from the planning activities.

In non-faith-based groups, the value of reflection, silence, and sharing is very worthwhile. The stimulus for the reflection could be words of the founder, reflections others have made on the work of the group, the way the organization has contributed to the life of the community, etc. A process similar to the one designed above could be adapted to all organizations to help them better understand that planning for a future helps build a better world.

Connecting with each other is essential to Prophetic Planning. One of the best ways besides prayer for connecting to each other is truly listening to each other—standing in the shoes of the other to really hear what is going on. We need to listen with the heart to hesitations, fear, hopes, and dreams. It is in truly listening and dialoguing about what is really important that the energies of the Spirit are unleashed and new ideas as well as new communions come about. It is a matter of not just listening for facts and figures, however important they may be. It is listening to the whispers of hope, the tears of sorrow, and the coalescing of forces needed to build the new reality.

As we listen and bond with each other, we can gradually let go of some of our poignant self interests and be open to new possibilities which will benefit the entire community. We come to a point in the process where what is really important surfaces—a point that all can agree on. As a group arrives at that point, and it comes after months of patient dialogue, then where one worships, or which buildings are used for a school, or where the central offices of the nonprofit move to, is not of the essential importance it once was. What is paramount is the vibrant existence of the organization.

The learnings for connecting on the journey include the interconnection between God, the transcendent spirit among us, and the deep bonding that we have grown into as a pilgrim community. For groups that are not faith-based, the connections on the journey come from a renewed ability to speak together with one voice, a new critical mass of "movers and shakers" now committed like never before to a positive vision of the future or a new way of working together for a shared common good.

Seeing, Naming, and Acting

On our journey, besides learning to listen deeply, we have learned to see, name, and act. Seeing with our eyes, seeing with our minds, seeing with our hearts, and seeing with our imaginations helped us understand planning in a new light. Our eyes are doors to our minds. Using our eyes in the Prophetic Planning process, we see data, numbers, trends, people, and events. When we see with our hearts, we recognize compassion, pain, hurt, sorrow, joy, and hope. When we see with our imaginations, we see beyond what we know. According to Albert Einstein, "Imagination is more important than knowledge… for while knowledge defines all we currently know and understand, imagination points to all we might yet discover and create." In Prophetic Planning, we are called to see and imagine everything that we could be and do to excel at our mission. At times of diminishing resources, it is a temptation to get stuck on all the things we can't do, instead of imagining something new and creative that we can do.

Naming what we see can be a powerful experience. First of all, naming it for ourselves helps us to understand the quandary we may feel we are in. Anxiety is often produced by the discomfort of not being able to name our feelings, not being able to describe where we are on the journey, or feeling too depressed to care. Words have power. Naming our realities helps us to deal with them. Not being able to name something contributes to the uncertainty of the future and the anxiety of the present.

Naming has the power to help us clarify our thinking in groups. We use one word or phrase or concept in a group and it either resonates with the group and helps the group articulate its position or passion, or it doesn't. If it does not assist the group, it is an opportunity for others in the group to suggest other words that may name the reality better. Such give and take bonds groups and shows the benefit of group effort. Naming can also challenge individuals in groups to contribute and to let go. "Wordsmithing" in groups can be difficult and trying at times. Often, once the concepts are agreed upon, a small subgroup is best suited to do final or near-final editing of documents.

Acting on what we saw and named is the purpose of planning. Plans which stay on shelves are useless. Action plans point to how goals and objectives and ultimately the prophetic vision can be accomplished. Action plans have a level of specificity and accountability which are needed for organizations to thrive and grow. Steps in implementing the organizational plan are often systemically integrated in staff performance goals, thus ensuring the effectiveness of the plan.

Prophetic Planning is a journey of growth, of new insights, of letting go, of grieving, of new relationships, and of creating the new. The journey promotes individual growth in new understandings and skills, as well as group development. Groups mature in the planning process.

Just as the Israelites started on their journey through the wilderness as a disjointed and disoriented group of people, they emerged out of the desert as a people who knew they were God's people, who knew what their mission was, who could articulate their values and had a vision of what the Promised Land would be like. The same God who led the Israelites and who led Jesus out of the desert and ultimately to his death and resurrection in Jerusalem, leads us through the many wildernesses of our lives. Prophetic Planning recognizes this presence with reverence and anticipation of the Spirit's continual nurturing. Thanks for being part of the Prophetic Planning journey. "May the God of hope fill you with all joy and peace in believing, so that you may abound in hope by the power of the Holy Spirit" (Romans 15:13).

For Discussion and Sharing

1. What surprises have you encountered in this book on Prophetic Planning? Where have you felt empowered to be a Prophetic Planner?

2. In what ways is planning a continual process? How can you develop a mentality of looking at various things you are involved with as part of a continuum of planning? What is the advantage of looking at your organization through the lens of planning?

3. What do you anticipate to be the biggest stressors on the planning journey, and how do you intend to deal with them?

4. What are the key connecting points for you on the planning journey? How will you make sure you are connected?

5. Name three new understandings about Prophetic Planning which you hope to put into action on your planning journey.

Resources

Periodicals

Myers, Gordon and Robert Boyd. "Grief Work: A Social Dynamic in Group Transitions" in *Personal Transformation in Small Groups*. London: Travistock/Routledge, 1991.

Scharmer, Otto. "Addressing the Blind Spot of Our Time, An Executive Summary of the New Book by Otto Scharmer: *Theory U:Leading from the Future as it Emerges*" (Cambridge, MA: Society for Organizational Learning, 2007). www.theoryU. com.

Scherer, John J. "Stride: The Breakthrough Process," *The 1986 Annual: Developing Human Resources*, J. William Pfeiffer and Leonard Goodstein. San Diego: University Associates, 1986.

Transforming Challenges, a monthly e-letter from The Reid Group. www.TheReidGroup.biz.

Books

Block, Peter. *The Answer to How is Yes*. San Francisco: Berrett-Koehler Publishers, 2002.

Bridges, William. *Transitions*. Addison-Wesley, 1993.

Cloke, Kenneth and Joan Goldsmith. *Resolving Conflicts at Work*. San Francisco: Jossey-Bass, 2004.

DePree, Max. *Leadership is an Art*. New York: Dell Publishing, 1990.

————. *Leadership Jazz*. New York: Doubleday, 1992.

Dogmatic Constitution on the Church, The Pastoral Constitution on the Church in the Modern World, Decree on Pastoral Office of the Bishops in the Church. *Vatican Council II, The Conciliar and Post Conciliar Documents*, Vol. 1 (New Revised Edition). Flannery, Austin, OP, ed. Northport, NY: Costello Publishing Company, 1996.

Enright, Robert D. and Joanna North. *Exploring Forgiveness.* Madison, WI: University of Wisconsin Press, 1998.

Fullan, Michael. *The Six Secrets of Change.* San Francisco: Jossey-Bass, 2008.

Hamm, Dennis, SJ. *Let the Scriptures Speak: Reflections on the Sunday Readings.* Collegeville, MN: The Liturgical Press, 2001.

Hiesberger, Jean Marie. *Fostering Leadership Skills in Ministry: A Parish Handbook* (Updated Edition). Liguori, MO: Liguori Publications, 2008.

Hughes, Patricia M. *Gracious Space.* Seattle, WA: Center for Ethical Leadership, 2004.

Kline, Peter and Bernard Saunders. *Ten Steps to a Learning Organization.* Arlington, VA: Great Ocean Publishers, 1998.

Kotter, John and Da Cohen. *The Heart of Change.* Boston: Harvard Business School Press, 2002.

Markham, Donna. *Spiritlinking Leadership.* Mahwah, NJ: Paulist Press, 1999.

Myers, J. Gordon. *People and Change: Planning for Action.* Madison, WI: Oriel, 1998.

Moltmann, Jurgen. *Hope and Planning.* New York: Harper and Row, 1971.

Patterson, Kerry, Joseph Grenny, Ron McMillan, and Al Switzler. *Crucial Conversations: Tools for Talking When Stakes Are High.* New York: McGraw Hill, 2002.

Preskill, Hallie and Tessie Tzavaras Catsambas. *Reframing Evaluation Through Appreciative Inquiry.* Thousand Oaks, CA: Sage Publications, 2006.

Quinn, Robert. *Deep Change: Discovering the Leader Within.* San Francisco: Jossey-Bass, 1996.

Ramshaw, Gail. *Treasures Old and New.* Minneapolis, MN: Augsburg Fortress Press, 2002.

Scott, Susan. *Fierce Conversations.* New York: Berkley Books, 2004.

Senge, Peter, Charlotte Roberts, Richard Ross, Bryan Smith, Art Kleiner. *The Fifth Discipline Fieldbook.* New York: Doubleday, 1994.

Senge, Peter, Charlotte Roberts, Richard Ross, George Roth. *The Dance of Change.* New York: Doubleday, 1999.

Senge, Peter, C. Otto Scharmer, Joseph Jaworski, Betty Sue Flowers. *Presence: Human Purpose and the Field of the Future.* New York: Doubleday, 2008 (Paperback edition).

Sofield, Laughlan and Carroll Juliano. *Collaboration, Uniting Our Gifts in Ministry.* Notre Dame, IN: Ave Maria Press, 2000.

Spencer, Sabina and John D. Adams. *Life Changes: Growing Through Personal Transitions.* New York: Paraview Press, 2002.

Stone, Douglas, Bruce Patton, and Sheila Heen. *Difficult Conversations: How to Discuss What Matters Most.* New York: Penguin Group, 2000.

Weldon, Michael. *The Struggle for Holy Ground*. Collegeville, MN: Liturgical Press, 2004.

Wheatley, Margaret. *Turning to One Another*. San Francisco: Berrett-Koehler Publishers, 2002.

Wheatley, Margaret. *Finding Our Way*. San Francisco: Berrett-Koehler Publishers, 2005.

Whitney, Diana and Amanda Trosten-Bloom. *The Power of Appreciative Inquiry*. San Francisco: Berrett-Koehler Publishers, 2003.

Zogby, John. *The Way We'll Be: The Zogby Report on the Transformation of the American Dream*. New York: Random House, 2008.

DVDs

Dialogue: Now You're Talking! Four program series, approximately 25 minutes each. We can all benefit from learning the tools of *dialogue*—how to communicate across differences in a way that is both respectful and effective. Available from Quality Media Resources, http://www.qmr.com/products/dialogue/.

For the Love of It and *Celebrate What's Right with the World*, 25 minutes each. Dewitt Jones discusses how we all have the ability to love what we do through honoring our passion, making a contribution to those around us, and expressing gratitude. In the second DVD, Dewitt, a *National Geographic* photographer, brilliantly portrays the value of being open to things far beyond our expectations. Star Thrower, 26 E. Exchange Street, Suite 600, St. Paul, MN 55101; 800-242-3220.

Seeing Red Cars, 10 minutes. Laura Goodrich encourages audiences to focus on what they want instead of focusing on what they don't. By having a positive attitude and taking action, viewers will be motivated to move in the right direction for themselves and for their organization. Star Thrower, 26 E. Exchange Street, Suite 600, St. Paul, MN 55101; 800-242-3220.

We Are the Ones, 5 minutes. This is an inspirational and compelling short program embracing the concept of looking to ourselves for leadership and positive change. The film is based on "A Message from The Elders," Hopi Nation, Oraibi, AZ. Star Thrower, 26 E. Exchange Street, Suite 600, St. Paul, MN 55101; 800-242-3220.

Acknowledgments

Bernardin, Joseph L. *A Moral Vision for America.* J. Langan, ed. Washington, DC: Georgetown University Press, 1998. © 1998 Georgetown University Press. All rights reserved. Used with permission.

Kaye, Kenneth. *Workplace Wars and How to End Them: Turning Personal Conflicts into Productive Teamwork.* New York: AMACOM, 1994, p. 4. © 1994 Kenneth Kaye. Used with permission conveyed through Copyright Clearance Center, Inc.

Marsella, Anthony J. "The measurement of emotional reactions to work: Conceptual, methodological and research issues," *Work & Stress,* Vol. 8, No. 2, January 4, 1994. Reprinted by permission of publisher, Taylor & Francis Group, http://www.informaworld.com.

Moltmann, Jürgen. *Hope and Planning,* M. Clarkson, trans. New York: Harper & Row, 1971. Copyright © 1971 by SCM Press Ltd., London. All rights reserved.

Myers, J. Gordon. *People & Change: Planning for Action.* Madison, WI: Oriel, 1998. © 1998 Oriel Incorporated. All rights reserved. Used with permission.

Thich Nhat Hanh. *You are Here: Discovering the Magic of the Present Moment.* Boston: Shambhala, 2009. English trans. © 2009 Shambhala Publications, Inc. Used with permission.

Wheatley, Margaret J. *Turning to One Another: Simple Conversations to Restore Hope to the Future.* (Copyright © 2002 Margaret Wheatley) and *Finding Our Way: Leadership for an Uncertain Time* (copyright © 2005 Margaret J. Wheatley). All rights reserved. Reprinted with permission of the publisher, Berrett-Koehler Publishers, Inc., San Francisco, CA. www.bkconnection.com.

Wilson, George, SJ. *On Being a Prophet,* Loveland, OH: Treehaus Communications, 2004. © 2004 Treehaus Communications, Inc. All rights reserved. Used with permission.